The Journey to Me

A Personal Journey through Depression

Sheila Boyd Cook

All scripture verses are from the
King James Version
This book was printed in the United States of America.

To order additional copies of this book contact:

Sheila Boyd Cook
4006 Sweethome Road
Ashland City, TN 37015
615-519-5518

FWB
FWB Publications
Columbus, Ohio

Table of Contents

Sheila Boyd Cook

DEDICATION

This book is dedicated to my wonderful
husband Joe. You were with me every step of
the way through this journey and continue to be right
by my side. I could not have gone through this experience
without
your love, compassion and dedication.

My Journey With Depression

Author's Preface

Many of us spend our lives on journeys in search of different quests. A journey usually means travelling from one place to another for a rather long time. We spend our lives seeking ourselves, careers, family, health and happiness. My journey finding me has seemed like a destination beyond my reach. Along my journey of life, I was diagnosed with severe depression which stopped me in my tracks. I call it my unexpected cross to bear. Walt Whitman, in Leaves of Grass says, "Not I, nor anyone else can travel that road for you. You must travel it by yourself. It is not far. It is in within reach. Perhaps you have been on it since you were born, and did not know. Perhaps it is everywhere – on water or land". My life was amazing until 5th grade and the events that happened then and continued to happen changed me from that bright blue-eyed girl to someone just going through the motions.

As you will see from this book, depression can be a very scary thing and in my case life-threatening. Depression is real and if you are fighting this battle, you are not alone. Depression seems to have been the bane of many of life's great leaders. In the Bible, Moses, Elijah, David and Job all had to deal with it. In the secular world, Sir Winston Churchill called depression his "black dog" and Ernest Hemingway referred to it as "the artist's reward".

Due to the fact that I don't remember every detail of the first few days in the hospital, you will read excerpts from my journal entries and my husband's recollection of the process, along with Facebook posts, and recollections by my sister, mother and niece.

My actual diagnosis came in February of 2012, but journal entries from 2010 show the beginning of my experience with depression but I didn't recognize the warning signs. Soledad O'Brien once said, "I've learned that fear limits you and your vision. It serves as blinders to what may be just a few steps down the road for you. The journey is valuable, but believing can empower you to walk down an even brighter path. Transforming fear into freedom – how great is that?"

Don't confuse your path with your destination, just because it's stormy now, doesn't mean you aren't headed for SUNSHINE!

By no means is my journey complete, but every day I found myself closer to my destination. I believe in the miracles of God. Only he can turn a mess into a lesson, a test into a testimony and a trial into a triumph and a victim into a champion. I hope that from sharing my story, I will inspire and encourage others coping with the same issues and to transform that fear into freedom.

Chapter 1

On February 8, 2012, I woke up like every other Wednesday morning and began my daily routine. While getting dressed, I felt faint and dizzy, but just thought it was from the medicine I had taken for the migraine. Anyone who suffers from migraines know how I was feeling. Since the age of 16, I have been dealing with migraines and they seemed to be getting worse as I get older. I remember walking into the bathroom to finish getting ready and that's when I felt myself going to the floor. Joe found me in the floor when he came home from work. My two yorkies, Sir Winston and Duchess were laying right beside me. I don't know how long I had been there but he got me up, made sure I had not hurt myself when I fell and put me to bed. That is the benefit of having a paramedic for a husband. Once in bed, I immediately went to sleep and according to my husband I slept until the next morning. I really don't remember anything about that Wednesday or the next few days that followed.

Facebook posts from my husband:

February 9, 2012 – "I brought "She" (that is what he calls me) to the ER this morning, she has had a migraine since Tuesday of this week and I found her passed out on the bathroom floor yesterday when I came home from work".

February 10, 2012 - "We are still at Vanderbilt Hospital. For you that are not aware, Sheila has had migraines for years but Wednesday morning I found her passed out on the bathroom floor. She went to bed and when she woke up she couldn't remember anything that happened. The doctor said to take her to the ER. While in the ER, she has a "spell"... not an actual seizure but she wasn't sure of her surroundings, didn't recognize her family, or even the fact that her father had passed away in 2005."

February 11, 2012 – "Sheila is not any better at this time, as a matter of fact, she is a little worse memory wise. I always tell her "I love you" from the day we met 10 years ago and her reply was always, "I love you too". Now I tell her and she just stares, but I want to believe that she is staring, "I love you too".

February 13, 2012 – "Monday Update: Saturday was her worst day thus far. She had no idea who several people were who came to visit her at the hospital. (They were immediate family). Joy, her daughter, stated after her visit, "That was the worst feeling in the world to see your mom but know she isn't there". Sheila seems to be reverting back to being a child. She is asking for people she thought so much of as a child who have passed away and she is making childlike gestures".

To hear the anguish and fear in my husband's voice through his posts and my daughter's statement sends chills through my body. How did I get to that position? What led up to that hospital stay? Where was the woman that exactly one month ago had left Miami with her husband for a cruise on the Carnival Valor to the Western Caribbean? Where was the woman who parasailed and swam with the stingrays in Grand Cayman? Where was the woman who had driven through the villages of Honduras and relaxed on the beach? Where was the woman who had been shopping in Belize and enjoyed massages? And where was the woman who soaked up the sun's rays at the Island of Passion in Cozumel? Would that woman ever return?

The emergency room visit is a little foggy to me. The feeling I was having reminded me of being in a dark cold basement and unable to get my bearings. It is like driving in a severe snow storm and not knowing where you are because you lose all sense of direction. I do remember going to the hospital and Joe standing by my bed. There were some other people in the room and a doctor. The other people in the room were lined up against the wall in front of my bed. I looked at them and told them to tell daddy to come on in. I kept asking for my daddy to come in the room. I just knew he was there in the waiting room. He was always there when I had been admitted into a hospital and what would stop him from being there today. We used to tease daddy about checking out the parking lot when one of us was sick. When I had my three children, daddy was always there but never came into the room until after the babies were born. He didn't like to see me in pain. When asked where he had been, he would always say he was checking out the parking lot. So I just knew that daddy was there that day waiting to see me. I kept begging the other people in the room to let him come in. Come to find out, the people lined up against the emergency room wall were my mother, sister, and daughter. That was when Joe told me that my daddy was not coming. Mother told Joe not to tell me, but he decided to tell me anyway. Joe told me daddy had passed away several years ago and asked if I remembered being the main speaker at his funeral. It was then I lost it and began to cry. According to my mother, I cried uncontrollably and started screaming. How could I have not remembered something as important as that? The one person I could count on in my life was gone and I didn't remember his passing. Things got worse from then on.

I had no idea what would be in store for me in the weeks to come. The hospital visit is a blur even though I was hospitalized for eight days. I do not remember the first four days at all. My husband, Joe had to tell me what went on and how I acted. For four days, I laid in a fetal position in bed with the sheet usually over my head. The only person I recognized from the start was Joe. I would not talk only stared the first few days. Maybe a nod here and there but no words. When strange people came into my room, I do remember telling them that my Daddy would be coming to see me soon. He was at work and when he got off he would be there. I did not remember that my best friend in all the world, my Daddy, had passed away in 2005. They tell me I didn't recognize my mother, sister, daughter or niece. How that must have made them feel. I didn't even remember that my daughter was getting married in a few months. The people I loved the most were there for me and I didn't even recognize them. It broke my mother's heart to see me laying in the hospital bed with no memory. She thought she had lost me for good. No one in our family had ever been through something like this and everyone was scared to death.

From what I understand they spent days running tests, everything from an MRI to CT scans and drew countless vials of blood. They had planned to do a spinal tap but decided to hold off on that because I was too restless. All those tests came back normal. Every day the doctors would tell Joe that they did not know what was going on, but they were going to get to the root of the problem. They were trying to rule out a stroke. The doctors even began to wonder if I had contracted something while in the Caribbean.

I do remember lots of people in my room from time to time, but didn't recognize any of them. One day a woman came to visit and she made me laugh. This woman had a young girl with her and they brought spa items into my room. I had a really bad headache and this woman thought being pampered would help. She placed cucumbers on my eyes and told me to relax. I remember telling her she was so funny and I was laughing out loud. This was the first time I had responded with laughter or even showed any signs of emotion. Come to find out the woman was my sister, Christi and the young girl was my niece, Savannah. Joe said I kept telling everyone that came to visit that my daddy was on his way. They said I would smile when I talked about daddy. It still hadn't sunk in that Joe had already told me several times that daddy was not coming and had passed away. Every time I talked about daddy, it upset my mother even more. She was really upset when

I didn't recognize her when she talked to me. I thought my Aunt Muriel was my grandmother, who had died several years ago. When she came to visit, I asked her if my Papa was with her and she said no. During those first few days, no one knew how to respond to my questions about people who had passed away. Many times they said they would just agree with me or tell me that they would not be coming today.

Around the fifth day, my memory slowly began to return in pieces. By this point, I was beginning to recognize people and was making conversation. I recognized my grandchildren, Noah and Ruthie, when Joy brought them to see me. She was a little apprehensive about bringing them because when she left the day before I was in a bad shape. But that day I had made a complete 360 degree turn and was recognizing everybody and talking.

Thursday, February 17th is the day I will never forget. My doctor came into the room and sat down at the foot of my bed. She told me and Joe that every test that could possibly be run had been and they all came back normal. Then she said that my problem was psychiatric. She believed I was severely depressed and my body was beginning to shut down. By getting me to the hospital when Joe did, probably saved my life. She recommended that I be admitted into the adult partial hospitalization at the Vanderbilt Psychiatric Hospital. What did she just say? I never thought in a million years I would ever hear those words, "You are a psych patient". She went on to say that she did not recommend me staying in the program overnight and being locked up so to speak. I would only go during the day and return home at night. I began to weep as she continued to speak. I held Joe's hand and said, "I'm sorry". He hugged me and said, "We'll get through this together".

Later that afternoon, a psychiatrist entered my hospital room and wanted to talk. I didn't have much to say, so I mostly listened. I was not use to sharing my feelings with people, especially strangers. He assured me that they would take care of me and help me through this stage in my life. I was not so sure at this point because I didn't understand what stage of my life I was going through. He prescribed several medications and explained that they would help. He left the room and I looked at Joe with total disbelief. I was a psych patient. I remember the floodgates opened up and I began crying uncontrollably. This could not be happening to me. My doctor returned later that afternoon while making her final rounds. She told me I was being released from the hospital and would start at the adult partial hospitalization at the Vanderbilt Psychiatric Hospital on Monday. Joe walked her to the hallway. I remember getting out of bed for something and falling to the floor. Joe and the doctor came rushing in and got me back on the bed. The nurses preceded to strap me in the bed with an alarm. From that point on when I tried to get out of bed an alarm would go off. At that point, I felt stripped of all my dignity.

I was released from the hospital later that evening, and I must say it felt good to be going home. Emotionally I was scared and physically I was exhausted. The last eight days, my body had been poked with needles and endured endless tests. My dogs, Sir Winston and Duchess would be waiting for me and I could not wait to hold them. When I entered the house, I felt a strange feeling. It was cold and made me shiver. I was almost scared of being home where everything had started. How was I going to cope? Would I ever get well? Joe told me everything would be alright and put me to bed to rest. I remember sleeping until the next morning.

The next morning, Friday, February 18, Joe and I had an appointment with the Vanderbilt Psychiatric Hospital to fill out paperwork and get me checked in for Monday. I had no idea what adult partial hospitalization was or what it involved, but I was about to find out. I was scared to death and the longer we sat in the waiting room the more anxious I became. A gentleman met me in the lobby and began showing me around the facility. I was actually having to do this, me in a psychiatric hospital. Everyone there was very nice and we spent time talking to the therapist who explained the routine. I would be in the facility from 9 a.m. until 3 p.m. Monday thru Friday. Breakfast and lunch would be served in the cafeteria each day. My treatment would last at least three weeks maybe more. I would be assigned to a physician who would manage my psychiatric treatment. The nursing staff would monitor my overall health and well-being. A social worker would be assigned to me and would be available to address individual, group psychotherapy, family and community needs as I needed them. I was given a schedule of the daily meetings and told I was required to be at all meetings. The man told me that I would check-in each morning upon arrival and have my blood pressure checked and talk with the nurse. The day would begin with a meditation reading of the day. Each patients would be asked to set daily goals and discuss weekly goal attainment. I would receive medication education to help understand the reasons for taking the medications and a basic understanding of how the medications work. There would be a group on coping skills that focused on self-help techniques to deal with negative emotions such as depression, loss, anxiety and anger. They would emphasize the identification of positive coping mechanisms and relationships. He went on to explain that patients would examine and discuss interpersonal relationships such as family relationships and the different roles we play and gain insight into how family dynamics create and reinforce these roles. As he talked, I began to be overwhelmed and began asking myself if I could do what he was asking. My heart began pounding and I had to tell myself to just breathe. He said there would be many other group topics discussed and that the treatment would end with participation in a group to develop and discuss hope, personal empowerment, social inclusion and personal meaning of life. Half of the things this man was saying to me made no sense. I didn't know what psychotherapy was and at this point I wasn't so sure I wanted to know. It all seemed a little weird to me.

As I walked through the facility, I saw patients of all ages. There were children there the same ages as the students I had taught. Some of them had such sad expressions on their faces. We walked passed the cafeteria and there sat patients in their pajamas just staring down at their food. The loneliness and defeat showing on their faces. These patients were in the inpatient treatment program where they stayed overnight. The gentleman explained that they treated all types of mental illnesses in the facility. Right then and there, it hit me that I was not alone. Others were experiencing the same pain I was feeling. What if the outpatient program did not help me, would they then lock me up in this place? My emotions were all over the place by this time and I just wanted to get out. I wanted to find the nearest exit door and run as far away as I possibly could. The therapist showed me the back entrance I would use every day to enter the building for my treatment. As we left the facility, I began crying and I could not stop. I had feelings of anger, pain and resentment. Why was this happening to me? My life had been sitting in a pew every Sunday morning, Sunday night, and Wednesday night. I was a member of the youth group growing up and when I became an adult, I was the youth leader. I attended the National Association of Free Will Baptist each summer and youth camps and now I found myself wondering where God was at this particular moment. I was a preacher's daughter for goodness sake and a business leader in the community. This could not be happening to me. On that day, I found myself so far from God that it made me sick. Where was God? I prayed and it felt like my prayer did not go past the ceiling. Why would God let anyone go through such pain? The pain I was feeling was so real. The hurting in the chest, cold, clammy feeling was all very real. My head began to pound. I was mad at what had caused me to be in this condition. At the time, I had no real idea what that someone or something was, but I was being assured they would find out. My real journey is about to begin and I am scared to death.

My Journey With Depression

Chapter 2

The weekend felt extremely long for me. I kept thinking about going to treatment and what all the man at the facility had told me. I had feelings of anxiety, fear, and hopelessness. Joe kept reassuring me that I would do great and that there was nothing to worry about. I was still very exhausted from the hospital stay and stayed home the entire weekend resting. Saturday and Sunday were uneventful, but then it seemed Monday was here and I was going to have to begin a journey to recovery. Recovery is a scary word for me. I have heard about drug and alcohol addiction recovery and recovery from a health situation, but I was on a journey to recovery from severe depression.

It was day one of treatment. As I prepared to get dressed, I looked at myself in the bathroom mirror and thought to myself, "Who are you?" Without the makeup I saw a frightened, sad woman who feels like her world has been turned upside down. For years the makeup seemed to hide the scars, sadness, pain and despair I felt. But now, this very moment, I saw the real woman that was really staring back at me. She definitely needed help. I was, for the first time, admitting that I needed help.

The drive to Nashville from Ashland City seemed to take forever. Joe had to drive me because I was not allowed to drive. We made very little conversation. I think he sensed my anxiety. My emotions were all over the place this morning. I had so many questions. What was the treatment going to be like? Who would I meet? Would this really help? Even though I was nervous, I had a feeling of relief. Maybe now I would actually find what I needed to live a full life. Maybe now the scars would be healed. The scars that I had been hiding all my life.

When we arrived, I remember taking a deep breath and Joe said it would be alright. He kissed me and I got out of the car. As I walked to the courtyard gate, my heart began racing. Could I walk through this door? I clenched the gate handle, took one glance back at Joe who nodded and winked and I took that first step and walked in. The gate slammed shut behind me and it startled me. The next door I entered was the main facility door. I know once I opened that door there was no turning back.

I made my way to the first office down the hallway where a counselor welcomed me and immediately started to put me at ease. Blood pressure check was next before entering the group therapy room. I was directed to the lounge that was filled with fruit, muffins, juices and all kinds of snacks. I grabbed a muffin, banana and a juice box and made my way back to the meeting room. By 9 a.m. there were 15 patients assembled for the day. Chairs were arranged in a circle and I remember thinking, it was like an AA meeting. Though I had never attended such a meeting, I had only heard about them or seen them portrayed in movies. As we went around the room, people stated their first name and the reason they were in group. One by one they stated they were here for bi-polar disorder, grief, depression, drug and alcohol abuse, suicidal thoughts, and it went on and on. There was an attorney in the group who had lost his practice and his family, because he was diagnosed as being bi-polar. The lady sitting next to me was a nurse who also was diagnosed with bi-polar disorder and her job was in jeopardy. An elderly woman was dealing with the loss of her husband. A teenage boy was suffering from depression. When it came my turn, I wanted to get up and run but I stated my name and explained that I was there for severe depression. To say those words caused chills to run down my spine. I was suffering from severe depression and I was actually sitting in this group about to share my inner most thoughts. The oldest in my group was 80 and the youngest was 17. The people in that room were hurting and I was one of them. As I looked around the room, I noticed the sad expressions and tears. Did I look that sad? Was my countenance that of a severely depressed woman? I thought I had been doing a good job of putting on that smile every morning and acting like nothing was wrong. If the truth be known I probably could have won an Oscar for best actress in a real life drama.

Each day began with a meditation reading and today the reading talked about self-esteem. The counselor quoted Margery Williams who said, "You only become real when your fur has been rubbed off". Self-esteem is the reward for peeling away our fakery, looking squarely at our character defects and building on our strengths. What is real in life is gloves-off, go for broke involvement. The gloves were coming off and I hoped to peel away everything that had caused my depression to show itself. I was going to be actively involved in my recovery and I wanted so desperately to be well. Peeling away our fakery and looking closely at our defects was something that scared me to death. For years I had hid those things from myself and others. Now I was going to have to take a close look at myself and learn to build on my strengths. Today, I only see the negative in my life, where have all the positive thoughts gone?

After mediation readings we were asked to state our emotions or how we were feeling. Another morning routine would be to set SMART goals for the day. SMART goals are specific, measurable, attainable, realistic and timely. Setting goals for myself was a little unusual, but after a few days it became natural. My goals, on day one, were to walk 30 minutes, letting go of hateful resentments, and drink more water. Pretty good for a first day, don't you think. My SMART goals each day gave me a specific activity to do and strive to achieve. After all, I would be doing this for at least three weeks, so I might as well start on day one setting goals and making a sincere effort to achieve them. With goals set, it allows me to schedule activities within my day that allows for no down time. Down time always got me into trouble. That was when I would feel sad, anxious and defeated and usually ended up in bed. Down time always led me into the kitchen where I would graze.

This first day I learned that depression is nature's way of getting us to slow down, stop and deal with our feelings. Depression had definitely stopped me in my tracks. We must acknowledge sadness, pain and hurt and give ourselves permission to feel them. Wow, that definitely hit home for me. It is not that what happened in my life was ok, but it is the letting go of it and moving on that will lead to a healthy person. But how was I to do that? I had so much pain and resentment bottled up inside me that I had been drowning in it for years. There were times I felt like a buoy floating out at sea being tossed back and forth with the waves. Were they going to teach me how to let go and move on? I couldn't wait for that lesson.

We were asked to keep a journal starting today about our feelings and the events going on in our life. Journaling has become a necessity for me to actually express what I am feeling since I usually keep my feelings to myself. Sharing feelings is something I have to work on. Journaling for me each day relieves stress, helps me heal, and lets me know myself and the truth better.

This is my journal entry for February 20, 2012 Day 1 of treatment:

"As the makeup is removed, I am seeing how events in my life have made me the way I am today: unhappy, tired, depressed, fatigued, overweight, to name a few. I have made my share of bad decisions along my life's journey. You would think the consequences would have made me stronger with an ability to cope better. Hopefully, with this partial hospitalization at Vanderbilt, I will learn coping skills to help me. First day of therapy was exhausting but refreshing. To be able to share my feelings with people in the same situation and to be understood by counselors is an amazing feeling. For the first time in a long time,

I see hope, I feel what I say really matters. I truly believe God has given me a second chance at a great life. I am finally seeing that maybe I do deserve to be happy and healthy".

"Deserve to be happy" were words I have said before but never truly believed them. When looking for a journal to take to therapy, I came across a journal from 2010. I began to read the pages and as I read it became clear to me that my depression was beginning to show its ugly face back then and I didn't recognize it at the time. I began to cry as I read page after page. The weekend of March 15, 2010 I had a lot to say. That weekend I had packed my bags and left by myself on a trip to Gatlinburg. Things were beginning to trouble me and I needed to get away by myself.

My journal entry for March 15:

"9:30 p.m. – Arrived at Bent Creek Golf Village in Gatlinburg later than I intended. Ended up working at the funeral home until 2:30. But I am here now. Some may say I am running from my problems – I see this mini vacation alone as a way to find ME! The past five years have been one roller coaster after another and for my own sanity, I have to step off the ride for just a little while. Daddy's death was very traumatic for me and I still have problems dealing with his passing. I feel I have had to put on that smile, as I have always done, and go on. Daddy was my best friend in all the world and life is not the same without him. I feel people expect me to deal with it and move on. As a little girl, I was always Terry Boyd's daughter, the preacher's kid who, in the eyes of the church members, was to do no wrong. For 47 years I did what I thought would make daddy proud of me. I needed his approval. Aside from being Terry and Sue's daughter, I am a mother to Joy, Joseph and Terry. When their father and I divorced, they became my entire world. I worked hard and with my parents help, we made it. The day I got my teaching degree was the happiest day of my life. For once, I had finally accomplished something I wanted for myself.

Even though it was a sacrifice for the kids and myself, it was worth it. I was a success. I did something on my own and not on the coat tail of my parents. With that accomplishment, I still had feelings of guilt for doing what I wanted to do. When in the classroom teaching, I was in my own little world and loving it. Then came grandchildren and wow they are amazing! The sound of the word "Nana" coming from their lips is awesome. After six years of being divorced, I had decided that God's plan for my life was to be a teacher, single mother and grandmother. But in 2002, God blessed me with a wonderful man, Joseph. Our meeting was definitely orchestrated by God. From the minute I saw him, I knew I would marry him. Our first date was February 5, 2002 and on February 15, 2002 he proposed and on July 12, 2002 we were married. So my life changed again from just teacher, mother, grandmother, to wife, mother, teacher, and grandmother. I truly believe that God sent Joe to me when I needed him the most: to deal with my father's illness and death. As dad's health grew weak, we talked one day and he was worried about leaving mother. I promised Daddy that I would do whatever I had to do to keep the business from being snatched from Mom. When I made that promise, I never knew I would have to give up my teaching career for more than five years. But a promise is a promise. There are days that I resent my sister's ability to live her life the way she wants. Great job, good salary and time to spend with her family. But my life has been put on hold. As I write this, I become teary-eyed because I feel it is so unfair. I feel I am stuck in a job that brings me no joy and ties me down. Don't get me wrong, I love helping people especially during their time of need. The job has its rewards and I truly love all the families that I have been privileged to work with. The pressures of managing a funeral home are hard to handle sometimes. I feel like I do it all – manage, meet with all the families, do all the paperwork, direct services, and worry about finances. That is more than one person deserves to have to deal with every day. Then there is the fact that I have to deal with death, grieving families and sadness day in and day out. I WANT HAPPINESS! Does that make sense? Is it too much to ask? There are days I dread going to work and feel that my headaches are stress related. I also feel that my weight gain is influenced by my unhappiness".

March 16: "What a peaceful night's sleep. What is it about the mountain air that seems to bring rest and peace? It is beautiful here as I sit on the porch of the condo. Birds are chirping and the creek ripples in the distance. Aside from a few cars passing, all is quiet. My devotion this morning was Philippians 4:1-23. God must have known what I had been thinking and why I took this trip. Of course he knows my heart and thoughts, He created me. The verses spoke to me more today – my life is filled with worries and anxiety. Anyone felt that way? There have been days lately that I just wanted to scream, cry (I did that), and run as far away as possible. But reading the devotion made me realize to rejoice in the Lord always. Did Paul really mean always? But he said it again "Rejoice!" Rejoice when so many things are happening to me and my family? Rejoice that my daddy is gone? Paul didn't stop with rejoice – he goes on to remind me that "The Lord is near". Prayer isn't something I had to do, but rather something I get to do. I can bring all my worries and problems to God through prayer. So I must make everything (my concerns, worries, uncertainties) known to God. I am able to do this because God is near. The scripture says not to be anxious for anything for He is near. WOW! I have been so busy trying to stay afloat that I left God out of the equation. How does a person who was brought up in church all her life, a preacher's kid even, get so far away from God? Dear God right now I ask you to renew my spirit. My desire is to become a fresh, vibrant and alive Christian once again. It is time I take my eyes off myself and place them totally on you. Thank you for prayer and the ability to come to you with my concerns. As I look around me right now I see just how great you are and how content and happy I should be. Thank you Jesus for allowing me this time away from my day to day life to take time to renew myself mentally, spiritually and physically. Amen. It is time to take a walk. My physical being must be addressed also. I want to be attractive to God, my husband and my family. Let's get those tennis shoes on and get going!

March 17: "My last full day here and I feel it was worth the trip. It was worth saying I am going to do this for me. What have I learned about myself?

1. I have been going through the motions of being happy. I have done what people expected me to do. I became so overwhelmed with things that I was losing control. This made me angry inside with everyone. I am not happy! It has occurred to me these few days that I can change that. I should be able to express my feelings. I have to express my feelings and if the people around me won't accept that, then they must not want what is best for me. So I may make some people mad, but I feel they will eventually understand. If they love me they will.

2. I want more out of life – I want to enjoy living. This means taking time aside from work, husband and family for me. I need two hours a day for exercise, devotion and me time. I owe that to myself.

3. I want my marriage to be like it was when we first met – laughter, sharing, dreaming and getting goals for our lives.

4. Financially I want peace. Finances have played a big role in the problems we have been facing.

5. I want to be happy at my job. If that means moving on to something else, so be it. Dad knows that I kept my promise to him and have done more than most would have done. So I am at peace with myself for that. The only problem is mom's happiness. I don't want her to feel I have betrayed her and left her alone. I believe it is time for all of us to move on from the funeral home business. These days have shown me that I want to be better. I know I can and I will be better. So my words to all of you is PBPGINFWMY! (Please be patient, God is not finished with me yet)."

See what I mean. I sounded distraught and even angry at times in the words I wrote and that was two years prior to my hospitalization. That weekend getaway really didn't accomplish what I set out to do because I had to return to work on Monday and life continued as it had up until that point. It all sounded good. The journaling did help me put my feelings on paper. But I was never able to express those feelings to my family. It seems that when I am away from home and away from family, I can let go of my feelings and express what I am really feeling. I am hoping that treatment will help me open up more with my family and not allow me to keep those feelings bottled up inside. This treatment and therapy is my only hope to heal.

My Journey With Depression

Chapter 3

I arrived back to therapy this morning feeling anxious, tired, and a little dazed for some reason. I slept better last night, so I am not sure why these feelings. It almost seems that I am dislocated from the real world. I am going through the motions, but seem to be getting nowhere. My life seems like a big beautiful home with numerous rooms all decorated with lavish furnishing, but I'm stuck in the cold dark basement. I know that outside the basement walls, a beautiful life exists. I hear laughter coming from upstairs and people enjoying themselves. So why do I feel so trapped in the basement? Why can't I simply walk up the steps and enter the beautiful home? It is almost like the stairs are missing and I am stuck in this basement for the rest of my life. I see no way out. I feel so alone.

The meditation reading continued on self-esteem. This road to recovery is like any pursuit of treasure, it requires risk. Little progress will be made if our first concern is to avoid disappointment. In spite of our discouraging past experiences, we need to try again. We are all worth the effort. The counselor told us that perseverance is the passage to improved self-esteem. There is a Jewish proverb that says, "He that can't endure the bad will not live to see the good". I have endured the bad so I am now waiting to see the good. This facility and these professionals are here for me and they are going to help me find "me".

Session one was on the topic of anger. Boy, do I need this discussion. I feel so much anger and it scares me to death. I have always heard that anger can kill you. The counselor began by telling us that we have three choices when we feel angry. First, we can stay miserable. Next, we can change the stressor and finally we can cope with it or accept it. To do all of that we must first build awareness of feelings and behaviors. There is that word again – feelings. I am aware of my feelings but I do nothing about them. I can say for sure that I have stayed miserable too much of my life. I didn't know it was caused by stressors and that there were ways of coping with them and accepting them. Change the stressor is something I don't know how to do. When there is so many stressors in your life, how do you begin to change them? How do I change my job, family, just life in general? This therapy thing has a lot to teach me I can see that already. I was taught today that by journaling and spending time alone and being honest with myself about why I act certain ways will help build that awareness of feelings.

Healthy boundaries mean knowing and understanding what our limits are. We cannot set good boundaries if we are unsure of where we stand. The lesson today explained that we all have to identify our physical, emotional, mental and spiritual limits. What can we tolerate and accept? What make us feel uncomfortable and stressed? By answering those questions, it will be easier to identify what our limits are. We also have to set boundaries with other people without hurting their feelings. I hate knowing I've hurt someone. Fear, guilt and self-doubt are my biggest potential pitfalls. I always feared the other person's response if I were to speak up or say no. Because of that, I now feel drained. So how do I get the courage to sit my family down and set boundaries? Can I actually sit my mother down and tell her I am miserable at the funeral home? Can I sit my sister down and tell her I'm jealous of her life and feel that it is unfair that I have to work at the funeral home and she doesn't? How am I going to get the courage to sit the family down and have this type of discussion? The thought of that makes me physically ill. I hate confrontation and I believe that it will only be a confrontation. Boundaries are a sign of self-respect. I must give myself permission to set boundaries and work to preserve them. Setting boundaries is not something I believe is easy for anyone, especially me.

I don't believe my family realizes the seriousness of my condition. They are so used to seeing me take the lead and looking strong on the outside that they have never thought me to be so miserable inside and so vulnerable. The day I stood before hundreds of people at my father's funeral and spoke was the one of the hardest days of my life. But yet I stood strong for the family. Right before the funeral service was to start, my sister said, "I can't go through this". I told her she had to go through it and to get up and find her seat in the chapel. Again, I took the lead. I felt dad's presence and it was like he said, you can do this. So I walked to the podium and began to speak. To this day, I don't know how I managed to do that without breaking down.

Things are about to change. Things have to change. I have to make them realize there are days that I am going to need "me" time. I can't be the "yes" person anymore. Others are going to have to get out of the dugout and take a swing at the ball. There have been many times in my life when I wanted to stand up and say no, but was afraid of confrontation, so my no always became a yes.

Session 3 today was on coping skills and how not to get to that low point. Lately, all my points are at low on the rector scale. We were to list activities that we could do when we began feeling down or depressed. My coping skill was to just go to bed and avoid people and the problem. The counselor suggested activities or hobbies, set a schedule for activities and make sure there is no down time. My list looked like this: cross-stitching, yard work, going to yard sales/flea market, spending time with the grandchildren, exercise or take a walk, scrapbooking, play outside with the dogs, read a book, go on a picnic, mini-vacation with husband, etc. Other activities might be getting a manicure and/or pedicure, massage, lunch with my mom, sister or daughter. Once I got to thinking about it, there were a number of activities I can do when I feel down. Scheduling these activities into our day allows us to always have a plan. Over the years, I have made excuses for not doing these things. I'm too tired when I come home from work. I need to do this or I need to do that but never included things for me. So actually scheduling time in my day for these things might just work. I will schedule them in my appointment book and act as if it just another appointment that I must attend.

In this program we have so many therapy sessions going on all day. Recreational therapy today consisted of playing Scattergories. Why was I sitting in a room of sick people playing a game when I really wanted to get well? How was this game going to heal me? The therapist explained that games are a great way to get the mind off our problems. After a few minutes, I was having fun and so were the other patients. For a few minutes, we were able to take our minds off our problems and why we were here and just have fun.

During the last session today, I realized how relaxing meditation tapes are and how they erase the bad thoughts. The soft flowing music seemed to transport me to a safe place and I could feel myself relax and my breathing slowing down and I felt at peace. I made a note to stop at the bookstore on the way home to purchase some of these tapes to have at home. There are so many wonderful meditation tapes available at your local bookstore. I strongly suggest that you relax with one of these tapes. Three, that I highly recommend, are "Stress Reduction & Creative Meditations" by Marc Allen and "Mediations for Morning and Evening" by Bernie S. Siegel, M.D., and "Sleep" from The Relaxation Company. Since being in the program, every afternoon I arrive home exhausted, I go to my bedroom, put on a meditation tape and lay on the bed for about 30 minutes. It seems to transport me back to peace and gives me strength to complete the rest of my day.

I met with the psychiatrist at the facility today before going home. He started by wanting to know about my childhood. At first it was a little awkward talking about me to someone, but once I started it seemed to get easier. It isn't easy for me but I realize that I have to do this to gain closure to some things and move forward. He then asked me what led me to this facility. The question took me by surprise and I didn't have an answer. He asked me again and I began to cry. I mean I was sobbing and couldn't stop. It was the first time I had shown this much emotion since my hospitalization. Why was I crying like a little baby? This man must think I am really a basket case. But he moved a little closer to me, handed me a tissue and said, "It will be alright". There was no pressure to continue to talk, but to sit in the silence. He said that when I was ready to talk, he would be there to listen. In that moment, I knew I was in the right place and that I was going to get the help I needed and deserved. He walked me back to the group for the last few minutes of the day.

Journal entry for today: "February 21, 2012 – Day 2 of treatment: Encouraged by today's program. Still new to me and hard for me to express exactly how I feel. I want to get well so bad and I want it now! But I now realize that in order to get my good life, I have to travel this journey on my own. Praying that my family will understand and be patient with me. I do feel guilty for having to leave work on someone else's shoulders. But, I have to do this for me. If I say it enough maybe I'll get comfortable with the idea. Hard for me to feel worthy of "me" time. The topic of anger therapy was very eye opening. Realizing that I can practice ways to cope with certain feelings is comforting. The angry chart was very helpful for me to gauge my emotions. There have been times in my life when I was full of rage, but did not deal with my anger. Thus my coping skills began, the migraines became worse. I coped by keeping secrets and not coping. That was what made me snap. That is what led me to being a "psych patient". I have to schedule "me" time. I met a mother of two today who was very sick. She felt she would never be well. It was so sad to see the despair and fear in her eyes. I can relate to that fear of hopelessness and despair. There is nowhere to hide from life. So tired after the program, that it was naptime for me when I got home. Able to open up more with Joe. He is so supportive and understanding. I see how concerned he is for my well-being and I know he is as scared as I am going through this journey. I thank God every day that I have him by my side to reassure me that I am doing the right thing. Joe is walking on egg shells right now because he is afraid that something will trigger my relapse and send me back into the hospital. He is protective of me and wants the very best for me. It is very hard for me to talk about me, my feelings and why I believe I deserve a happy life. I am going to work to consciously every day to get to a place in my life where I truly believe I am worthy. I am seeing for the first time that putting myself first gives me the energy, peace of mind and positive outlook to be more present with others and to be there for them. When I am in a better place, I can be a better, wife, mother, co-worker and friend".

Chapter 4

My goals this morning were to start letting go of hateful resentments about my sister and work, to journal one page and exercise 30 minutes. Don't get me wrong I love my sister. She is amazing and I know she wants what is best for me. I don't guess I should use the term 'hateful resentments' when it comes to my sister. Resentment really comes from being taken advantage of or not appreciated. It is often a sign that we are pushing ourselves either beyond our own limit because we feel guilty and want to be that good daughter, sister, wife and mother, or someone else is imposing their expectations on us. Today when I look back on my resentment, I see that I allowed people to take advantage of me. I led them to believe that I could do everything and didn't mind doing it. It was easy for me to look at Christi, my sister, and say look at her life, look at her great job and look at her ability to go and do as she pleases. Most of my resentment was from throwing myself a pity party and dwelling in my own messes. I would have liked a little help in managing the funeral home, but I never asked for help. I want Christi to know I love her and never wanted to hurt her in any way or say things that would cause her pain.

The meditation reading this morning was on solving problems. Many of us lived in situations where it wasn't okay to identify, have, or talk about problems. Therefore, denial became a way of life – our way of dealing with problems. A problem doesn't mean life is negative or horrible. Having problems doesn't mean I am deficient. Everyone has problems to work through. Recovery does not mean immunity or exemption from problems; recovery means learning to face and solve problems, knowing they will appear regularly. Having problems doesn't mean that God is picking on us. Some problems are a part of life; others are ours to solve, and we will grow in necessary ways in the process. This treatment has taught me to face and solve today's problems. I do not need to worry needlessly about tomorrow's problems, because they will appear, we will have the necessary tools to solve them.

Emotions today are anxious and upset. Blood pressure was good and I am ready for the day to begin. Session one today was about the Johari Window. The Johari Window is a communication tool used to understand one's relationship with self and others. It is a model of self-awareness and personal development. Understanding relationships and how personality is expressed would be explored in this group. There are four boxes like panes in a window. One box is Open – it is facts that you share with others about yourself. The next pane is Blind – things that are not known by you but others see in you. The next pane is Secret – things we have kept secret and tell no one and the final pane is Unconscious – other's observation about us that hasn't been seen before. The more we put in the secret box the unhappier we become. We will have unhealthy relationships with self, family and others. Oh no, my secret box is so full and I have a feeling it is about to be opened whether I like it or not. Once we begin talking about secrets and listening to what others see, the unconscious becomes evident. This Johari Window is making sense to me now. But here comes the tricky part. Before we leave the program, each one of us will have to sit in the "Johari Chair" and share with the group. Oh no you are not going to make me sit in front of the group and share my feelings. I can't do that. Then the counselor explains that some may have apprehensions about sharing their feelings because if we unload too much, relationships may end and so we continue the cycle of don't talk, don't feel and don't trust. She then said we would listen to two people a day until everyone had a chance to sit in the Johari chair. As I sat there I thought I'll wait till the last day and maybe she will forget that I had not gone. I was having trouble sharing things with my husband and family much less sharing with complete strangers. But that's not really true. These strangers had become family to me in a very real way. They were seeing life through my eyes and I was seeing it through theirs. We had created a bond that nothing could break.

When rating myself today I gave myself a 4. Worse than yesterday because I was upset that my sister who I found out thinks my depression is not as serious as the doctors believe. She told my husband that I had acted this way before and was alright. Christi has a way of making light of things when she is scared and not sure what to do. My son is the same way. If they can make people laugh, then everything will be alright. That only brings on denial and nothing is ever solved when we are in denial. But I decided that I would focus on me and not what other people think. It is only their opinion. I will work on journaling and write down how this makes me feel.

Session 3 was on interpersonal effectiveness: objective, relationship and self-respect effectiveness. I am hearing some of these terms for the first time in my life and feel that I have so much to learn. Objective effectiveness is how good we are at asking for what we need and how easy is it to say no. I have already told you that saying no is not in my vocabulary and I certainly don't know how to ask people for what I need. For years I have put other's needs before my own. I am the caregiver and want to make sure everyone is happy. My father once told me that only clowns and fools try to make everyone happy. Relationship effectiveness is how good I am in keeping good relationships and leaving hopeless relationships. Since I am on marriage number two I would have to say I'm not perfect in relationships. Self-respect effectiveness is do I feel good about myself and how do I want to feel about myself after interaction with a person. In most of the relationships I have had, I was always worried about what they thought of me. Would they like me for me? So many times, I would act the way I thought they wanted me to act so they would like me. That got me nowhere fast. I have a hard time trusting individuals. People we can trust are people that listen without judgment, have an ability to respect one's privacy and have shared experiences. I am beginning to see that I have been looking at the world through a lens created by experiences. The experiences in life have made me the person I am today. Let me say here that not all my experiences were good to say the least.

Journal entry for today: "February 22, 2012 – Day 3: I have failed to see options and any possibility of letting go. I tell myself to stop the pity party- I need to work on me and forget what others think or feel. In time, I can only pray they will come around, but if not, I can only work and change me. Not sure why I feel so bad today. I am tired, overwhelmed and just want to sleep. Sleep – that has always been my coping skill. I thought that if I went to bed, I could just forget the bad and not have to talk to anyone. My bedroom has become my safe place, I don't have to talk to anyone, see anyone and can just be by myself. Even as a little girl, my bedroom was the safest place to me on earth. No one could hurt me there, no one could call me names, physically harm me and mentally abuse me when I was in my safe place. Lord, help me see the positive today. I feel like I am drowning in my feelings right now. After hearing the Johari Window, I realize that my secret box is overwhelming, overstuffed and running over. At least I recognize my secrets play a vital role in my problem and recovery. WOW! Today's therapy was amazing. Very eye-opening. Our meditation for today was on solving problems. Denial has become my way to solve problems. Denial means we didn't let ourselves face reality, usually because facing that particular reality would hurt. It would be a loss of something: trust, love, family, perhaps a marriage, a friendship, or a dream. And it hurts to lose something or someone. I see denial as a shock absorber for the soul. It prevents us from acknowledging reality until we feel prepared to cope with that particular reality. I will face and deal with reality on my own time schedule, and when I am ready. I spend more time reacting to a problem than I do solving it. I am learning that recovery can only come with facing the problems and events in my life and cope with them by sharing with others and let them go FOR GOOD! Easier said than done. The Johari Chair this afternoon really hit home with me. As patients shared their experiences, I began to cry. I wanted to fix all their problems. What was I talking about, I couldn't even fix my own problems. The love I have for these people is real. These people have lost all sense of hope. They believe that there is no way out. Not only do I want to get well, I want to see every one of them overcome the illness that led them to this place. I saw that I am unhappy because of all the items in my secret box. Over the years, I have placed items one by one in the secret box thinking that if they were out of sight, I could forget about them. Boy was I wrong. That only made the problems worse. While I thought by hiding them I was protecting those I loved, I was only killing the real me in the process. I now look forward to participating in the Johari Chair before I leave the program. Did I really just say that? Philippians 4:13 comes to mind: "I can do all things through Christ which strengtheneth me".

My Journey With Depression

Chapter 5

Arrived at therapy a little early this morning and had a chance to reflect in the quiet of the room before others arrived. As I look around the room and see the empty chairs, I see the individuals who sit in those seats. The lawyer, the nurse, the grieving wife, the mother, the teen-ager, all of them were on my mind this morning. I believe that when God places a person in your thoughts, He is wanting you to reach out to that person. For a moment, I prayed for each of those people and prayed that today would be a good day for them and me. See, there I go again thinking of others first. I don't suppose that is always a bad thing. It is my belief that God can use me even in the circumstances I am in today. I woke up this morning feeling down and had a heaviness in my chest. I still feel unhappy. But as the other patients enter the room one by one, I began to feel much better and the tightness in my chest went away. I am beginning to see just how important these people are to me and how they are a part of my recovery. God has definitely placed me with this group for a reason.

Meditation reading this morning was on recognizing feelings. Experiencing feelings can be a challenge if you have had no previous experience or permission to do that. Learning to identify what we're feeling is a challenge we can meet, but we will not become experts overnight. Nor do we have to deal with our feelings perfectly. We were given some ideas that would be helpful in recognizing and dealing with feelings. You can keep a diary, write letters you don't intend to send, or just scribble thoughts onto a note pad. Our body is a good judge of what we are feeling. Is it tense and rigid with anger? Running with fear? Heavy with sadness and grief? Dancing with joy? In recovery, we are on a continual treasure hunt. One of the treasures we are seeking is the emotional part of ourselves. We need to be honest, open, and willing to try. Our emotions are there waiting to share themselves with us.

Session one this morning was on communication styles. We are either passive, aggressive or assertive. Before the discussion begins I already have a feeling I can label my style. But let's wait and see the characteristics of each one before I give my final answer. The passive person was discussed first. This person doesn't stand up for their rights. They are people pleasers and their body language is usually head down and no eye contact. The passive is soft spoken, excessive head nodding, low self-esteem, lacks confidence, sad, lonely, dissatisfied and feels unloved. The Aggressor is a dominant person who intends to win. They use "you" statements and usually walk around with their hands on their hip, loud, pointing, direct eye contact. The aggressive feel insecure, feel slighted, defensive, angry and self-righteous. On to the Assertive individual who stands up for rights in a way that preserves respect and dignity for self and others. They speak clearly, make eye contact, understandable, listens attentively and are even tempered. The assertive is confident, good self-esteem, caring and nurturing. They take charge but are not controlling, able to say no and not feel guilty about it and are firm in their beliefs. Well, I was right, it was right there slapping me in the face, Sheila you are a passive person. Don't I know that the characteristics fit me to a T? But I don't want to be passive, I want to be assertive. To say the characteristics of the assertive person makes me feel good inside. Confident, good self-esteem, caring and nurturing, now that is the type of person I want to be. Just think how much more people would like me if I were assertive. Would it really help? God must have made me to be passive, right. Wrong. God created me in His image. This passive person was created by the experiences that have led up to this point. So my goal is to begin working toward being an assertive person.

I spent a long time with the psychiatrist today, I opened up more with him and began to tell him of the events in my life. As always, I began to cry telling him my feelings. Over the years, I had controlled the urge to cry. Crying was a sign of weakness, I told myself. Since being in the program, my tear ducts have certainly been emptied. It is a good feeling to let go and feel that cleansing. I told him I felt ashamed and unworthy to be loved. My feelings of anger have controlled me for so many years and I chose to do nothing about them. Then my psychiatrist told me that past decisions and past events do not define me. That made me sit up and listen. He also told me that when we keep something so tight fisted there are only nail prints, but when we open our hand and let it go, the wounds will heal. I had been holding those secrets in so tight that my wounds could not heal and that is what led me to the hospital. That is what led me to this facility and these people. I finally get it.

Journal entry today – "February 24, 2012 Day 4 of treatment: Discovered today that I am definitely an extreme passive individual and need to learn the skills to become assertive. Role playing today helped me see how I can change my behavior and body language in certain situations. Very hard to see me as aggressive or assertive, and I quickly fell back to my comfort zone of being passive. It is just easier for me to back away and say nothing. Therefore, I become a door mat for others who are assertive. I feel that my ignoring things or not saying anything or expressing my opinions or wants that everything and everybody will be ok. Which only makes me feel worse. I physically hate confrontation, it makes me physically ill, literally. So I would do whatever it took to prevent it and now I am suffering. Everyone else seems to be living a happy life and I am in this cloud. Leaving that comfort zone is scary to me. I do not expect to be happy overnight, but I need to continue to take the baby steps to full recovery. What will people think of me? Will they look at me differently? Last night, I took a big step by posting on Facebook my diagnosis and being in treatment. Joe said he was proud of me, but I am scared. People's responses were all very positive. I was a business leader in my community for goodness sakes and when people hear about my problem, will they not trust me, will they take their loved ones to another funeral home? Will they pity me, will they lose faith in my ability? Again it is hard not to worry how other people feel and think about me. Why can't I get past that? Personally I think it comes from my preacher's kid syndrome. The preacher's kid syndrome is when you live in a glass house and people are always watching to see if you mess up or do something wrong. Afraid that if I am not perfect, I am bad. After therapy today, I came home and walked 30 minutes. Finally accomplished one goal this week. As I walked, the sunshine and wind on my face made me feel good inside. As I looked at the beautiful white clouds, I became sad and started to cry. I want to feel free to float carelessly among God's creation. Even in the midst of feeling good about walking, I feel pain and sadness. Will the black clouds hovering over my life ever end or disappear? I am learning it is in my hands. Do I really feel I am worth the work to be happy? My family deserves an upbeat and happy wife, mother, grandmother, daughter and sister. What do I deserve? Hmmmm – that's a hard question for me to answer. People tell me I am worth it, but I feel that I have so much work to do. Will they support me and still be around when I have recovered? Guess I am afraid of being alone. It is very hard for me to say, I deserve a better life. This comes from past events – being yelled at, hit on the head every day, locked in a closet every day at recess by a 5th grade teacher all because I had trouble with my multiplication; or being dumped by my first love; being molested every day for 6 months by a man in our church; being in a verbally, mentally and physically abusive marriage for 13 years and then the loss of my very best friend- my father. Why wouldn't I feel worthless? How many people survive these things and feel great about themselves? I feel sick to my stomach, dirty, embarrassed, guilty, worthless and lonely. The reason I stayed in an abusive marriage for 13 years was because I felt no one else would want me. That was the reason I was single for 6 years after my divorce; who would want me and truly love me and why did I deserve to be happy? I spent 6 years taking care of my children, going back to school and received a degree in Elementary Education. When my Dad, my rock, passed away my life literally fell apart. My heart had been ripped out of my chest. Even though, at that particular time, I had been married to Joe for three years, the only man who understood me and loved me unconditionally was GONE! The problems began to surface, but I had to go right back to work after the funeral. I was told to be strong and go on. I had to suppress my true feelings to keep the business going. I had a funeral business to run and my dream of teaching was put on hold. I was still Terry Boyd's daughter, a preacher's kid, a teacher, a funeral director, a manager of a family business and in my spare time I was to be a wife, mother and grandmother. My family was a strong well-respected family in the community so to show signs of weakness would not be good. SO, the secrets and suppressed problems were covered once again like the bruises on my body in the abusive marriage. I was so used to putting on the makeup of a happy person that no one could even imagine what I was feeling in my body and mind then and now".

My Journey With Depression

Chapter 6

I wrote down that my emotions today were sad, down, a headache, tired and sleepy. My sleep patterns are getting better, so I am not sure why I am so sleepy all the time. The meditation tapes help me relax so that I can go off to sleep. The medication they have me on may be making me tired. The question asked us today was, "How are you feeling as this week ends?" Physically, I am a little stronger but tired. Mentally, I have a desperation to be well. I worry about my job and finances. Emotionally, I feel sad, anxious and in a fog most days. Will those feelings ever stop? I am beginning to wonder, but then this is just the first week of treatment. Spiritually, I need work on that aspect of my life. Prayer is very important to me now. The low point in my recovery process was realizing that I needed help. My high point was finding a safe place in the adult partial hospitalization at Vanderbilt. As I prepare for the weekend, I am a little sad that I will not be in this safe place. Here I feel cared about and loved for who I am. In treatment there is no reason to pretend that everything is alright. I feel that people actually want to help and care about my recovery. But I know that I am going to have to do a lot of the work outside of these walls. I have got to learn to cope with the outside world and all that it brings my way. This first week leaves me feeling more confident now, than I did five days ago, that this treatment will help me on the road to my recovery.

Setting our own course was the topic of the meditation reading this morning. We are powerless over other people's expectations of us. We cannot control what others want, what they expect, or what they want us to do and be. But we can control how we respond to other people's expectations. People may make demands on our time, talents, energy, money, and emotions during the course of any day. We do not have to say yes to every request. The most important thing is that we do not have to feel guilty if we say no. It is evident that we do not have to spend our life reacting to others and to the course they would prefer we took with our life. But we can set boundaries, firm limits on how far we shall go with others. It is important that we trust and listen to ourselves. This treatment has taught me that we can set goals and direction for our life. It is time to place value on myself.

Several patients sat in the Johari chair today and the experiences they shared were unbelievable. We cried with each other and at times laughed together. That is what is so special about this group therapy. We have become a family and when one is hurting, we all hurt. When one is happy, we celebrate with them. Even the smallest breakthroughs are celebrated. It still amazes me that mental illness can affect anyone. Lawyers, nurses, doctors, teen-agers, mothers, fathers, business men, business owners, the prominent and the poor can be diagnosed with bi-polar disorder, depression, grief and it can happen at any time. But we are there to give encouragement and listen. I feel a little more ready to participate in the Johari chair and I know my day is coming. What will I say? What will I reveal about myself? There is so much to tell that I have been keeping in my secret box that I am afraid that when I begin to share, I will not know when to stop. I guess I will know when enough is enough. The thought of actually sharing my secret box gives me a sense of relief. For the first time in my life, I will be able to release all those secrets and breathe a sigh of relief. The two key ideas of the Johari Chair is to build trust with others by disclosing information about yourself and with the help of feedback from others, you can learn about yourself and come to terms with personal issues. Hopefully, by disclosing information to my group, I would begin to trust others and ultimately be able to share the same information with my family.

The day was dismissed a little early and I was glad. We had planned a date night just the two of us and I was looking forward to getting out like we used to before my hospitalization. Mother came and picked me up this afternoon because Joe had to work. I was a little quieter than usual and mother was afraid that something was wrong. The therapy sessions are exhausting and I tried to explain to her what goes on during my day. I can tell she is worried and really doesn't know what to say to me. Everyone in the family is walking on egg shells around me and I guess afraid that I am going to snap again at any time. I feel for my family because I know they love me and feel like they want to help but don't know how. Families have to realize that it takes time during the recovery process. People don't get better after one week of treatment. Recovery is a day to day process. My life is filled with 40 years of secrets and issues and it will take more than a week or two to get well. My goal is to open up to them about my treatment and share what I have learned. They have to understand what happened and what caused my depression. I think it would be beneficial for families to participate in some of the therapy sessions to get a feel for what is going on and that there is a medical reason for these conditions. But I can't focus on them right now, I have to stay focused on my recovery and what I need to do to reach a point in my life where I can deal with the diagnosis of depression.

When I arrived at the facility a week ago, I was a broken individual filled with hopelessness. Many of us find ourselves in those dark moments when it is hard to find hope or figure out what to do next. Sometimes we feel hopefulness because of something that happens to us – we make a mistake, have to deal with a big disappointment, lose something or someone we care about, or have to deal with situations that are really stressful or overwhelming. My hopefulness was caused by all of the above.

Today, I feel some healing is taking place and don't feel so broken. I am still scared but confident in this process. The weekend scares me to death but I have to take one day at a time and do what I feel that I am able to do.

Journal Entry for the weekend: "February 24 – 26, 2012: Program today was good even though I am feeling crappy. Not sure what has caused this mood. The week has been exhausting and so much to learn. Each session is overwhelming but the things I am learning make sense. As we left the program today, everyone hugged each other and wished each other a good weekend. I am looking forward to date night with my loving husband. We saw the movie "The Vow". This movie reminded me of my memory loss and all I could do was cry. Needless to say, it was not the movie for me at this time in my life. It dawned on me that it easily could have been me who lost my memory for good. After the movie, it was off to Cheddars for dinner. My mood was down and I felt bad for Joe who was trying so hard to make this a great evening. My thoughts turned to my illness and suddenly I felt like everyone in the restaurant was staring at me, but I managed to sit through dinner. When you are depressed, you feel like there is a sign tattooed to your forehead that reads, "I am crazy". My husband assured me that I looked great and that no one could tell I was depressed. Very quiet on the way home and now I am on my way to bed. Sorry Joe, I promise I will make it up to you.

February 25: "Woke this morning at 9:30, showered and felt really good. Weather is beautiful. Joe and I plan on spending the day together. Our first stop will be to Hobby Lobby to get our formal portrait from our cruise stretched and framed. Every time I look at that picture, I see the smiles on both our faces. We were having so much fun on that cruise. The picture was taken on formal night on the cruise ship. Memories of that time bring a smile to my face. Joe looked so handsome in his suit and I was dolled up in my pretty little black dress. I felt very special that night and did not have a care in the world. Will those smiles ever return? The cruise was the happiest time in my life except for my wedding to Joe. No pressures, carefree today. After Hobby Lobby, it was off to Sam's for a few groceries and then return home.

Today, I drank my last coke. I am going to see how long I can stay off of them.

February 26: "Sick all day with a migraine. Stayed in bed all day. I think I overdid it Friday night and Saturday. I had planned to go to church today, but it didn't happen. Maybe next week. I know Joe was afraid things were going back to the way I was in the hospital. When I go to bed, it scares him and I can see why. Tomorrow has to be better! Tomorrow, I will be back at my safe place again and among friends.

My Journey With Depression

Chapter 7

It is Monday morning and my goal for today is to walk 30 minutes and drink plenty of water. Those things have been hard for me to follow through with, but I am trying. The emotions I am feeling today are anxious and a feeling of desperation. This is week two of my treatment and things are looking much better to me now even though I still have some anxiety. After talking to the psychiatrist this morning, I am opening up more and more without crying now. He told me that he could tell I was much stronger than I was when I first entered the program. I explained to him that I thanked God for bringing me to this place and for all the wonderful people that have been placed around me while in this program. Every day, the sessions are on topics that hit home to me and I have learned so much from them. Never in my wildest dreams would I ever think that I would be talking to a psychiatrist. I always thought they were for the extreme cases. I told him that today and he looked at me and said, "Sheila, you were an extreme case when you entered this building". While talking to him, I realized then and there that I would have to be seen by a psychiatrist once I left this facility. He told me that before I left, one would be appointed to me and I would see them on a weekly basis for however long they deemed necessary.

You are lovable. Yes, you and I. I am learning that lesson every day. It is still hard for me to say the words, but I am beginning to see that I am lovable. Just because people haven't been there for us, just because certain people haven't been able to show love for us in ways that worked, just because relationships have failed or gone sour does not mean that we are unlovable. We have all had lessons to learn. Sometimes, those lessons have hurt. We must let go of the pain and open our heart to love. I am the only person that I spend 24/7 with and if I don't like myself, it makes for miserable days. This particular meditation reading was important for me to hear and let it sink into my mind.

Session one today was on what we are going to allow in our life and what we are not going to let in our life that will get us down. For me, I used my job as my example. I told the group that I was unsure at this point when I would be able to return to work, but I needed a plan before I go back. The counselor told me not to go back until I was ready. But when will I know? She assured me that my body would tell me when I was well enough to cope with the job and the day to day stress. The group helped me devise a plan to put in action in regards to my job. I would delegate work to others. It would be important to schedule a time for me each day. Starting the day with meditation and devotion would be a good way to get the day on the right track. Another suggestion was to eat healthier and get plenty of sleep. Time management of my work, family and home is a big one that I desperately need to work on for my sanity. I think these suggestions are attainable and reasonable. The one good thing about group therapy is that people are able to help you see things in your life that you cannot see. I am able to see my life through their eyes. The group helped me see that there were things I could do to ease back into my job and not let the job get the best of me. My job had consumed my life and I was dying a little more inside each day. I was there to make families feel better in a terrible time in their life and all the while I was feeling terrible inside. At times I guess I was envious of those families who had the time to grieve for their loved one. The day after dad's funeral, it was back to work for me. The first death call I received was at the same hospital and in the same Intensive Care Unit that my dad had passed away. Talk about hard, I had to stand outside the doors for a while before I could face the family. I remember taking a deep breath and walked in and did my job. No one ever knew I was hurting inside and wanted to cry.

We then had to go around the room and share what we liked about ourselves. This is always hard or me. I find it uncomfortable to say good things about myself. So here I go with my list: good wife, good mother and grandmother, considerate of others, hard worker, good writer, educated, determined, good teacher, good listener, love the beach and I love to cross-stitch. Now that really wasn't all that hard. But when I look at the list I feel that I am being boastful and I shared that with the group. I was told that I was supposed to be proud of me and the accomplishments I have made in my life. It is alright to pat yourself on the back from time to time. The others in the group seemed to have a hard time with this task as well. Not many of us are used to bragging about ourselves or we don't see ourselves in a positive manner. Much of how we feel is caused by what we say to ourselves. We talk to ourselves all day long with little awareness of it. This is because self-talk is automatic and carried out repeatedly.

When we are not sure why something is the way it is, we often start looking outside of ourselves for the source of unhappiness or other form of emotional stress. We have the impression that what is happening outside of ourselves is what makes us feel the way we do. While there is some contribution from the environment or situation, it is also our thoughts and interpretation of the situation that causes or influences our associated feelings. Therefore, what we think about a situation is a big factor influencing how we feel and respond. The most positive aspect about this is that we have choices. With effort, we are able to notice the way we are thinking about life events and to make the choice to think about them in more realistic and healthier ways.

It is likely that if we do engage in negative self-talk, that we have been doing it for a long time. It may have even started when we were very young. It starts when we begin telling ourselves negative things about our life situation and ourselves. Not surprisingly, these types of internal messages can start when we are young because we are unhappy, a negative thing may be repeatedly said to us which becomes part of our identity, we didn't feel like we had control over our own life, and/or we have not been taught good coping skills. All of this makes it easier for us to externalize or blame the way that we feel and our responses to some entity outside of ourselves and our control rather than taking responsibility for our own feelings and actions.

As an adult all of this negative self-talk is seen as perfectionism, chronic worrying, always being a victim, self-criticism, low self-esteem, phobias, panic attacks, generalized anxiety, depression, and hopelessness. It is also possible to feel so bad emotionally that it affects us physically. For example: headaches, abdominal distress, intestinal disorders and frequent illness. That explains why my headaches have become unbearable and frequent. Examples of realistic self-talk statements are: this too shall pass and my life will be better, I am a worthy and good person, what is, is, I am not helpless. I can and will take the steps needed to get through this crisis.

Next, we discussed guilt. Guilt is one of the causes of depression. We have regrets and sometimes ask ourselves What if? We blame ourselves for events that happen beyond our control. Guilt also plays a huge part on low self-esteem. What actually causes guilt? The counselor gave us this list: lying, illness which impacts our life, change in behavior, letting people down, using the words: "should have", "could have" or "would have", feelings of worthlessness, addiction/relapses, and failure. To let go of guilt we have to forgive our self, recognize it as a feeling and that it is normal and spend time on our self. We should treat our self like we treat our best friend. How do you treat your best friend? There is respect, we want to take care of them, spend time with them, be honest, say positive things, be supportive, give them gifts and communicate. Those are the very things we should be doing for us. I never thought of myself as my best friend. But I guess if I don't take care of me who will, right. This all makes perfect sense to me now. I have to stop criticizing myself and replace those words with positive things. That's a tough one, but practice makes perfect. At least that is what they say.

Journal Entry – "February 27, 2012 Day 6: Back to program today for my second week. Today was a pretty good day despite the headache. I have decided that my headache is due to not having a coke in two days. At therapy today, I was able to share my 5th grade experience. Come to think of it this is where my first feelings of doubting myself came in to play. I was humiliated each and every day by Miss Martha because I had trouble with multiplication. Every day when I did not answer correctly, she would take a ruler and hit me on the head. During recess EVERYDAY I was locked in the coat closet and told I was stupid. Every day I heard those words and so did my classmates. I tried making myself sick to avoid going to school – sometimes it worked, but most days I would run after my Dad's car when he dropped me off at school, screaming to high heaven. From then my self-esteem was gone. It was then I began closing myself off from people by staying in my room and reading. Well, after all I was stupid right, so I had to read to get smarter so I could prove myself. By staying in my room and reading, people always made fun of me and told me I was a sad person who never smiled. They were right, I was sad. So now, I am feeling stupid, made fun of and sad. What a life! Why would I leave my room, my safe place – only to face ridicule? And to add to that I was a preacher's kid. It was as if I had "I am a PK" stamped on my forehead. The congregation was always looking at our family. It was almost like they tried to find fault. For example, Dad finally took my sister and me to a Disney movie and was criticized; I went to my senior prom and was criticized. So why not shut myself off from the world? My room and my bed seem to be the place to be. Being able to live would have been nice. Now while I am writing and sharing my thoughts, I will continue with the secrets that I have kept bottled up inside for all these years. Then my mother asked me one day in high school (senior year, I think) was something wrong, why wasn't I dating? There was only one boy I would have ever considered dating. He did ask me out and I thought I had found my soulmate. He walked out of my life unexpectedly. Again, I felt all alone – for three months I sat on the couch, not eating much, lost 30 pounds and sat waiting for him to return. He never returned. After recovering from that broken heart, I felt that something must be wrong with me. It was then I decided to go to work. I worked for a few months and felt that God wanted me to go to Free Will Baptist Bible College in Nashville. Strict environment so I could not possibly fail or let anyone down. A man in our church owned a printing company in Nashville and offered me a job for a few hours every day after school. I was excited to earn money. The first week went well then things changed. He began by having me stay later and would walk up behind me and massage my shoulders and back and told me that standing all day was stressful. It became a daily thing and led to sexual molestation every afternoon. He told me he was helping me become a woman and if I told anyone, my dad's job as a minister would be over. The guilt was enormous – here I was a Bible College student, a preacher's kid and the man doing these things to me was a church member. So to protect my parents, my church and my feeling of being dirty and embarrassed, I never told anyone. I didn't tell anyone until the day before I started the program. I told my husband. Burden #1 almost released. I know I have to tell my mom and sister. But that is such a big step. Afraid of rejection and blame. Will I ever be able to tell them? I am afraid they will hate me. So now I have two events to tell them about. I know that it will release a huge burden. My recovery from self-doubt will begin. Being in group has helped me see just how important it is to be more open and express my thoughts and feelings. Some of these things I plan on sharing during my time in the Johari chair. Sharing them in this journal first has helped me see that I really do need to get these things off my chest and release the burden that has been bottled inside of me for years".

Chapter 8

Have you ever stopped to think about how you communicate with people? To be honest, the thought had never crossed my mind until today. The topic of discussion was communication. We need to stop and think about what we say or think about people and our self. Our thoughts lead to emotions and emotions lead to behavior and the cycle continues. We develop lens from events that have taken place and that is how we view everything. I feel I can talk to most people, but I stay away from a lot of personal talk. I am afraid they will be able to see through me. Some of us see the facts based on how we feel. 'Should' statements such as "This is what a good daughter should do" makes us feel trapped and feel guilty. This is especially evident when we are overwhelmed. That is exactly how I view certain things in my life. My mind has been full of "should" statements and the way I view things is based on those feelings. Up until this point, I would say, "This is how a preacher's daughter should act", or "This is how a good daughter should respond to this situation".

Letting go of anger was the topic of our meditation reading today. In recovery, we often discuss anger objectively. Yes, we reason, it is an emotion we are all prone to experience. The goal in recovery is to be free of resentment and anger. It is okay to feel angry, we agree, right. Well, maybe. Anger is a powerful and sometimes frightening emotion. Anger is a warning signal. It points to problems. Anger signals problems we need to solve. It points to boundaries we need to set. Sometimes, it is the final burst of energy before letting go, or acceptance, settles in. It is refreshing to learn that we don't have to feel guilty whenever we experience anger. We can shamelessly feel all our feelings, including anger and still take responsibility for our behaviors.

Cognitive behavior therapy was a term that I was unfamiliar with and had no idea what I was about to experience. This type of therapy explores painful feelings, emotions, and experiences. The counselor warned us that all of us may feel emotionally uncomfortable at times but that would be normal. She went on to say we might cry, get upset or even feel angry during one of these sessions and we would feel physically drained. We were about to confront situations that I had been avoiding and had rather avoid. First, we were asked to identify troubling situations or conditions in our life. That was hard for me because there were several troubling situations that I could recall. Once we identified the situation, we were to become aware of our thoughts, emotions and beliefs about the situation. The situation that I identified for this session was the molestation by a church member. I became angry, and I felt ashamed and unclean. The counselor explored those feelings a little deeper and my anger became intense. I did not like feeling this much anger. My face became hot to touch and I felt dizzy and sick to my stomach. The last step was to identify negative or inaccurate thinking about the situation. In my situation, I had always felt that I caused the situation to occur. What had I done to cause this man to act this way? By the time, my situation was discussed, it was evident that I had nothing to do with the situation and that I had been blaming myself all these years. Negative or inaccurate thinking can cause a life of despair and hopelessness.

I have learned that there is no right or wrong way to feel. A feeling just is. Why do I bottle up my feelings? Why can't I say what I feel and be honest about those feelings? We bottle up our feelings because we are afraid of what others may think and we fear not being accepted by others. As a middle school student and on into high school, I felt I was different because I was a "preacher's kid". While other kids were wearing jeans to school, I was wearing a dress or skirt. I felt like I looked and acted different. Talking about things might bring up exactly why we feel the way we do. Yes, that nailed it on the head. Those are the very reasons I have lived my life with bottled up secrets and feelings. So what can I do when that occurs? I now know to acknowledge the feeling and allow myself to feel and ask myself "how do I want to react to it in a healthy comfortable way?" All these years I have been reacting in a way that has caused me so much pain and sadness. My depression has evolved because I did not react in a healthy way to my feelings. After so long, my body said enough is enough and came to almost a complete stop to get my attention. I never knew feelings and how we react to them could play such an important role in our life.

Session three today discussed mindfulness. Mindfulness is the ability to be aware of your thoughts, emotions, physical sensations and actions. In the present moment, without judging or criticizing yourself or your experience you need to be aware of what is going on in your mind. Be mindful of yourself and make an impartial observation of yourself and put words to it. Most of us never take the time to look at ourselves and make observations, especially putting words to describe it. This program has taught me to be more mindful of my present thoughts and emotions. I guess it is getting in touch with the real you. When we block out the world around us and see ourselves in a mirror, we see someone totally different. It is like when you remove the make-up and you see the real you. What are you thinking? How are you feeling? How are you reacting to the events of the day? I am learning to step back and see the real me for the first time in a long time. Sometimes it is not a pretty picture, but it is me. The real me — what does that look like? When I look in the mirror, I see a woman who has been through a lot in her life. It shows in the sad expression on her face. This woman has experienced good times and extremely bad times. I am afraid of not knowing if I will be able to cope outside of the program. There are people who love me, but I don't love myself. I don't see how anyone could love this woman staring back at me.

The woman I see can put on a smile at the right moment but be hurting inside at the same time. She has let the needs of others come before her own needs and desires. Not a very pretty picture, but I warned you it wasn't going to be pretty. By the time the program is over I hope to see a different woman looking back at me.

Journal Entry: "February 28, 2012 – Day 7 – In the program today we talked about effective communication. How do I communicate with people? We also discussed cognitive behavior therapy which is an approach used to discuss and assist with the identification of antecedents, behaviors and consequences of events. During this session we discussed our own beliefs and coping techniques. New coping strategies were introduced and discussed. I need to stop and pay attention to what I say and think about myself. Based on events in my life, I feel they define me. What I have really done is LET the past events define me. I have let "should" get in my way. This is what a preacher's daughter should do, this is what a good daughter should be or do. I am seeing that I do feel trapped and guilty. Today I was told there is no right or wrong way to feel. A feeling just is! That is liberating to me".

Chapter 9

Anxiety is a normal human emotion that everyone experiences at times. Many people feel anxious, or nervous, when faced with a problem at work, before taking a test, or making an important decision. Anxiety can cause such distress that it interferes with a person's ability to lead a normal life. It is healthy and necessary because it protects. But when it gets out of control it becomes debilitating. My anxiety level has been high for several weeks now. It seems the little things make be anxious and tend to throw my life into a spin. When there is high levels of stress that equals chronic levels of anxiety. There is a fight or flight response that comes into play with anxiety. The "fight or flight response" is our body's primitive, automatic, inborn response that prepares the body to "fight" or "flee" from perceived attack, harm or threat to our survival. In the fight response adrenalin is released into the blood stream, we experience increased respiration, blood rushes from internal organs to arms and legs, pupils dilate, awareness intensifies, sight sharpens, impulses quicken, we bypass our rational mind and fear is exaggerated and we tend to overact to things. When our fight or flight system is activated, we tend to perceive everything in our environment as a possible threat to our survival. By its very nature, the fight or flight system bypasses our rational mind—where our more well thought out beliefs exist—and moves us into "attack" mode. This state of alert causes us to perceive almost everything in our world as a possible threat to our survival. As such, we tend to see everyone and everything as a possible enemy. Like airport security during a terrorist threat, we are on the look-out for every possible danger. We may overreact to the slightest comment. Our fear is exaggerated. Our thinking is distorted. We see everything through the filter of possible danger. We narrow our focus to those things that can harm us. Fear becomes the lens through which we see the world.

We can begin to see how it is almost impossible to cultivate positive attitudes and beliefs when we are stuck in survival mode. Our heart is not open. Our rational mind is disengaged. Our consciousness is focused on fear, not love. Making clear choices and recognizing the consequences of those choices is unfeasible. We are focused on short-term survival, not the long-term consequences of our beliefs and choices. When we are overwhelmed with excessive stress, our life becomes a series of short-term emergencies. We lose the ability to relax and enjoy the moment. We live from crisis to crisis, with no relief in sight. Burnout is inevitable. This burnout is what usually provides the motivation to change our lives for the better. We are propelled to step back and look at the big picture of our lives—forcing us to examine our beliefs, our values and our goals.

The flight response is where we hold everything in and do not release our feelings. This leads to chronic pain, headaches, depression. It is exhausting and evidentially it causes us to snap. I had been living in the flight response all my life and it caused me to finally snap and collapse on the bathroom floor. When looking back at my life, I remember the day I had a severe panic attack but at the time I thought I was having a heart attack. I was teaching school and one day my heart began to race and I could actually see my heart pounding in my chest. There was shortness of breath and hot and cold flashes. I was scared to death. I thought I was going to die right there in my classroom. After managing to walk to the office, I told my principal that I think I needed an ambulance. Of course in our little town, when the ambulance is called, the fire department arrives first on the scene and entered the school in all their glory. The first one to me ordered IV fluids and immediately I was laying in the school clinic with an IV in my arm. The ambulance arrived a few minutes later and took over. By the way, did I mention that is how I met my husband? He was one of the paramedics on the call. I told him I thought I was having a heart attack and he assured me after checking my vitals that it was only a panic attack but they would be taking me to the hospital to rule out any heart issues. I was placed in the ambulance and taken to Baptist Hospital where I remained in ICU for a couple of days to rule out the worst. The paramedic sure got my mind off my pain and on to him. Later, he called to ask me out and we were engaged ten days after our first date. He always tell people that I faked a heart attack to meet him. He was right, it was only a panic attack, but scary just the same. This was the first time I had noticed that my anxiety had resulted in such a full blown attack. To this day, I have a fear of having another attack. So what can we do to avoid panic or anxiety? First, identify a safe place. My safe place is usually my bedroom. If I can just get to the bedroom and lay down, I seem to calm down. Second, medication can help avoid these attacks. And then learning deep breathing techniques will help us focus and slow our breathing back to normal. When we are out and I begin to feel panic, my husband can tell and suddenly starts to tell me to take deep breaths and concentrate on my breathing. It is all about retraining our body to act differently in these type situations. There are relaxation and visualization tapes and videos available to train your body to relax and breathe normal. Since my hospitalization, I have avoided crowds because I do not want to have a panic attack in public. If I do go out, I don't go alone because I want someone there to help me through it if I suddenly have an attack. There have been times when my family has invited me out to eat and I refuse simply because I don't want to face the crowd and worry about a panic attack. I have missed many an enjoyable time with family because of this fear. By the time I am through this program, I want to be able to handle any situation that comes my way.

It's day nine of my treatment and I am beginning to see everything in our lives make us who we are today. After the discussion about anxiety and panic attacks, we turned our attention on our thoughts for the day. My thoughts were on being a perfectionist; feelings of helplessness; feeling I am between a rock and a hard place and it is hard to see hope some days. I feel that some things are just unfair and I have unrealistic expectations. After sharing my thoughts and emotions with the group, I was reassured that my feelings were normal and that they too would pass. It is amazing how far I have come within the group since my first day here. I actually look forward to sharing and hearing what the other patients are sharing. Over the past few days, I have seen sad faces turn into smiles. When other patients experience their "ah ha" moment, we all celebrate with them. Today the attorney, I mentioned earlier, spoke for a while on his bipolar diagnosis and what had been happening in his life since he began the program. The first week he was here, he tried to end his life by driving his car into the path of a semi. But God had other plans for his life that day and preserved his life. He said that he felt like he was in handcuffs and the key had been thrown away. He had lost his private practice, his family and friends to this disease. The tears from his eyes showed a very hurt and distraught man who needed this program and us to encourage him to continue on this path. He and I left the program the very same day and we hugged each other as we walked to our cars. I reminded him that God loved him and that we both had to remember what we had learned inside those walls. My favorite line is "and this too shall pass". I shared that with him and we both had a laugh. The ability to laugh with each other is a wonderful thing. My prayer is that he is doing well and that God is using him to help others.

Journal entry: "March 1, 2012 – Day 9: No headache today. Was able to actually have a pleasant conversation with Mom on the way to and from therapy. I can't wait until I am able to drive *myself to therapy. I feel I am a burden to everyone. I am beginning to feel better and hopeful. To be happy is my goal today. Therapy was great, we talked about anxiety and panic attacks along with anger. Man, am I angry – suppressed anger got me to this place. Comments, jokes, mentally, verbally and sexual abused, terrible first marriage, daddy's death and on top of all that work stresses. Why wouldn't I be angry? Thought by suppressing my anger, I was coping. Dinner at Logan's with Joe tonight. I was able to finally open up to him. We actually spent over an hour just talking. I loved it and it felt great. He is my rock, protector and best friend. God knew just what I needed when to send Joe into my life. I thank God for Joe every day. We continued talking all the way home and my love for him grew".*

My Journey With Depression

Chapter 10

Day 10 of treatment, but due to tornado warnings the day was dismissed at noon. To say the least I was a little sad when the day was cut short. I have come to love the therapy sessions and the people in my group. When I leave the treatment facility, who will I talk to and share my feeling with? Where will my safe place be outside these walls? By the time I leave, I will have gotten the nerve up to talk to my family and express my needs and desires. Yeah, right that is only a week away. At least they say I'll be here another week.

Before we dismissed, we did have a meditation reading. Be who you are was the title of the reading. Sometimes, our instinctive reaction to being in a new situation is: Don't be yourself. Who else can we be? Who else would you want to be? The greatest gift we can bring to any relationship wherever we go is being who we are. We may think others won't like us. We may be afraid that if we just relax and be ourselves, the other person will go away or shame us. I am guilty of worrying about what the other person will think. When we relax and accept ourselves, people often feel much better being around us than when we are rigid and repressed. Do we need to let the opinions of others control us and our behavior? Giving ourselves permission to be who we are can have a healing influence on our relationships. The tone relaxes. We relax. The other person relaxes. Then everybody feels a little less shame, because they have learned the truth. Who we are is all we can be, all we are meant to be and it is enough. Our opinion of ourselves is truly all that matters. My prayer today is to relax and be who I am in my relationships Help me, God, let go of my fears about being myself.

I am looking forward to the weekend and time of relaxing. These therapy sessions take a lot out of you mentally and emotionally and it takes a weekend to rest up and prepare for the next week. This Sunday, I am planning on going to church for the first time since my hospitalization. That is a little scary, but I know that my church family has been lifting me up in prayer all this time. How will I look to them? Will they think I'm crazy? I guess I'll find out Sunday.

Journal entry: "March 2, 2012 – Day 10: This morning I woke up early to the sound of rain and thunder. Peaceful sound. I showered and spent 30 minutes in devotion, meditation reading and now journaling before going to therapy. I feel refreshed today. I think it was due to the time I spent with Joe last night. Looking forward to therapy today. I can see how each day gets better and I am able to share more. More importantly I am working on understanding what made me the way I am and why I have felt this way for so long. There is hope on the horizon! My blood pressure today was 130/80 which I thought was great. Severe storms are in the forecast and I worry about being away from Winston and Duchess. They are terrified of storms. Therapy started off with more frustration – loud and interrupting Kathy was back. Lord help me to get through the day without punching her or having a panic attack. She is such a distraction for the entire group. Everyone sits and looks at each other while she talks and rolls their eyes. Therapy dismissed at noon due to the tornado warnings. Joe picked me up. When I got home my cousin Donna needed help rounding up all 4 horses that had gotten out of the pasture. We spent 2 hours getting them back to their pasture. I am exhausted now, so back in the house cuddled on the couch with the dogs. Night of TV. Looking forward to the Home and Garden show tomorrow."

"March 3, 2012: Up and ready to hit the Home & Garden Show in Nashville and spend the day with Joe. I have come to love the time I can spend with him. Yesterday we weathered the terrible storms and today there is sunshine. Feels like my life, I am learning how to weather the storms of my past, accept them and move into the *sunshine. Home show was just what I needed. Walking through the gardens and waterfalls gave me a sense of refreshment and peace. Also being out in public was easier when I didn't know anyone. Came home and just relaxed on the couch watching movies with Joe. Wonderful way to end a beautiful day. Noticed I was playful today and laughing. What a change! I am learning to make decisions and do things "I" want to do."*

"March 4, 2012 – Taking a big step today – going to church. My mother's picking me up. Church went great despite my emotions and dread. Everyone was so supportive and the hugs meant a lot to me. Having a church family is so supportive. After church it was dinner with the family at my sister Christi's house. Great conversation and I felt a part of the family again. After dinner it was back to the Home and Garden show with mom, Christi and Savannah, my niece. Once back at Christi's we had leftovers and just talked. Conversation centered on my treatment. I was able to open up to them and tell them all the painful events of my past. A heavy burden was lifted. They were great about it. We cried and shared and they were so excited that I was able to share. Their support means everything to me. Looking forward to group tomorrow. My family was more than surprised when they heard all I had been through. How I had gone through all of it and had not mentioned a word to them. It was my way of protecting those I loved. I was going through it, so why should I drag them into this awful mess of a life. After listening to me for almost an hour, they all agreed that I needed to take all the time I needed to get my health on the right track. I also told them that I was going to have to schedule frequent "me" times and that they would have to be willing to fill in for me. It is an amazing feeling to share so much negative and have only love and support given back to you. Prayer was the most important thing I needed from them at this moment. I needed them to pray for me every day that my treatment would open my eyes and give me the tools I need to go on with my life. My prayer life has become so important to me

these last few weeks. Prayer was always in my life, but now I need it every day in my life to get through the day. I am sure the Lord is probably getting tired of me calling on his name. It's me again Lord needing your outpouring of love today. Isn't is an awesome thing to know we can go to him in prayer and he hears our every word. There are days when I need his loving arms wrapped around me and his sweet voice calming me. Getting through this on my own would have been impossible and I don't know how people who don't have the Lord survive these kinds of struggles".

Chapter 11

Life is difficult. I'm sure I didn't have to tell you. It is not easy in fact, it down right hard. Everybody wants to be happy in life. We all want to live the prefect life. We want that great job or a successful business. We want to be married to Mr. Perfect and Mrs. Perfect. We want to have great kids and friends that stick with us come rain or shine. We want to be able to have all the material things life has to offer and have all our problems just disappear. In the book, "The Road Less Travelled" M. Scott Peck begins with the words "Life is difficult". But as Peck goes on to explain, once you accept that life is hard, it no longer becomes an issue that it is difficult. He goes on to say "Once we know that life is difficult, once we truly understand and accept it, then life is no longer difficult". Life is hard – your boss will not always be the nicest person in the world. Your job will have challenges that you did not foresee. Your coworkers will sometimes be a pain. You won't always get the salary and recognition that you want and deserve at work. Life is hard – your kids will not always be the ideal kids you want them to be. Your home may not be the ideal place you want it to be. You may not be the perfect husband or wife you once thought you were. The bottom line is life is hard. You can say that again. My life has certainly not been easy.

Feelings on the job was the topic of our meditation reading this morning. Our feelings at work are as important as our feelings in any other area of life. Feeling are feelings and wherever we incur them, dealing with them is what helps us move forward and grow. Not acknowledging our feelings is what keeps us stuck and gives us stomachaches, headaches, and heartburn. I can say amen to that. My headaches were due to my feelings about my job. It can be a challenge to deal with feelings on the job. Sometimes, things can appear useless. My favorite trick to avoid dealing with feelings is telling myself it is useless. Feelings are to be felt and accepted. Most of the time, they are pointing to a problem in us, or a problem we need to resolve with someone else. Sometimes, our feelings are helping to point us in a direction. They are connected to a message, or a fear such as: I'll never be successful... I'll never get what I want... I'm not good enough... It is important to remember whenever we bring a spiritual approach to any area of our life, we get the benefit. We won't know what the lesson is until we summon the courage to stand still and deal with our feelings. Today, I decided that I must consider my feelings at work as important as my feelings at home or anywhere else. I have to find an appropriate way to deal with them. As manager of a family business, I never acknowledged my true feelings about my job and a part of me resented my job and the stresses it caused in my life. Learning to identify my true feelings is part of my recovery and I now have strategies to deal with my feelings.

I am learning to be mindful. The topic of mindfulness is discussed frequently in treatment and I believe for a good reason. Mindfulness means maintaining a moment-by-moment awareness of our thoughts, feelings, bodily sensations, and surrounding environment. Mindfulness also involves acceptance, meaning that we pay attention to our thoughts and feelings without judging them—without believing, for instance, that there's a "right" or "wrong" way to think or feel in a given moment. When we practice mindfulness, our thoughts tune into what we're sensing in the present moment rather than rehashing the past or imagining the future. When we are depressed, we are locked in the past. We are ruminating about something that happened that we can't let go of. When we are anxious, we are ruminating about the future -- it's that anticipation of what we can't control. In contrast, when we are mindful, we are focused on the here and now. Mindfulness trains individuals to turn their attention to what is happening in the present moment. Beating ourselves up for past experiences gets us nowhere. We must learn to just let what happened, happen and accept the present moment. Acceptance is not agreement and it doesn't mean it is pleasant. I don't have to agree with the events in my life but I have to accept that they happened and move on. I don't have to agree with the way Miss Martha handled my inability to remember multiplication facts and putting me in a closet, but I must accept that it happened and move on. It is not my fault that a man sexually assaulted me for six months but I do have to accept the fact that it happened and move on. I have to accept the fact that my father is gone and I have to move on with my life. Is it going to be easy? No, life is hard. We must stop fighting the feelings and accept them and do what works. If there is one thing I have learned through therapy is that there is always a way to deal with our emotions. We have to practice acceptance and believe you me it will take practice.

Journal entry: "March 5, 2012 – Day 11 – Woke up and had 'me' time with devotion, meditational readings. Joe drove me to therapy today. Shared with him how it made me feel to share with Mom and Christi yesterday. He said he was proud of me. Actually, I am proud of myself. I did something I never thought possible and it felt good – holding things in for 44 years took a toll on me. In my quest to protect everyone, I did not protect myself. I rated myself a 7 today. Yes I have come from a 4 last week to a 7 today. What an accomplishment! Spoke with the psychiatrist today and he says I am beginning to address my fears and acknowledging my past. I feel I am very close to exiting the program. It is an anxious feeling and the real work begins when group ends. But I am ready to be happy. My feelings today are very upbeat and it has been a long time since I have felt upbeat. Program was exhausting today. At the end of the day, we shared feelings – this got pretty tough for some. One young girl was so angry she wanted to kill her father. There are so many people here haunted by their past. Some things are just hard to let go of. After program, went to Publix for blood pressure meds. Ate supper

*when we got home and then it was time to relax on the couch and
watch a little TV. Didn't get my goals accomplished today. I was
so tired that I didn't even want to see Joy and the kids tonight. I
just needed quiet time".*

Chapter 12

It is day 12 and I am feeling pretty good about how far I have come in the program. Emotions today are running on tense and agitated. I am wondering if it is caused by the thought of me leaving the program. The fear of failing is haunting me and I don't want to end up back in the hospital. Have I learned enough during my stay here to keep me on the right track? What happens if I relapse and have to start all over again? Will the next time be worse than my experience this go round? My goals for the day are to walk 30 minutes and enjoy a long bubble bath tonight. I must say achieving my goals have been hard at times throughout the program, but by setting these goals I have a tentative plan for the day outside of program.

Meditation reading was on signals of new growth in our recovery. Shunryu Suzuki said, "Before the rain stops we hear a bird. Even under the heavy snow we see snowdrops and some new growth". The signals that new growth is underway we often very small at first. It's sometimes discouraging when we are trying to remake our lives and all we can see for our efforts is minor growth. That is how the natural world works, and we are part of this world. When the little sprouts of growth first develop under the snow in spring, we don't even see them unless we search. But they signal the beginnings of a total transformation. Time will bring vast changes, but only little signs are showing first. In recovery, I search for signs of progress in my life. The little things we see may signal bigger transformations yet to come. To be true to them in the long run we must accept them, even welcome them, as they are today. During my treatment at the facility, I have noticed the subtle movements toward health and renewal in my life. I have realized that welcoming them will encourage them.

Session one was on sleep hygiene. I can't remember the last time I had a good night's sleep. It is nothing for me to get out of bed 4 or 5 times a night and just walk around the house. My counselor said the most common cause of insomnia is a change in our daily routine. For example, traveling, change in work hours, disruption of other behaviors (eating, exercise, leisure, etc.) and relationship conflicts can all cause sleep problems. Paying attention to sleep hygiene is the most important thing you can do to maintain good sleep.

The list of do's on the sleep hygiene list include:

- Go to bed at the same time each day
- Get up from the bed at the same time each day
- Get regular exercise each day, preferably in the morning
- Get regular exposure to outdoor or bright lights especially in the late afternoon
- Keep the temperature in your bedroom comfortable
- Keep the bedroom dark enough to facilitate sleep
- Use your bed only for sleep and sex
- Take medications as directed
- Use relaxation exercise just before going to sleep (muscle relaxation, imagery, massage, warm bath, etc.)
- Keep your feet and hands warm.

The don't list includes:

- Exercise before going to bed
- Engage in stimulating activity just before bed (playing a competitive game, watching an exciting program on television, or having an important discussion with a loved one)
- Have caffeine in the evening; read or watch television in bed
- Use alcohol to help you sleep
- Get to bed too hungry or too full

- Take another's person's sleeping pills
- Take daytime naps; and command yourself to go to sleep (this only makes your mind and body more alert).

If you lie in bed awake for more than 20-30 minutes, get up, go to a different room, participate in a quiet activity such as reading, and then return to bed when you feel sleepy. Do this as many times during the night as needed. I have found that the relaxation CDs help me relax enough to go off to sleep most nights.

Found out today that I will be leaving the program in two days. Friday will be my last day for partial hospitalization, my last day to talk and share with the friends I have come to love. The last day to walk into this facility and learn from these wonderful people. I don't want to leave. To be honest, this is now my safe place. Here I feel good, I feel refreshed, I feel alive even among all the hurting people and me being one of them. Deep down I know that I have learned coping skills that will help me on the road to my recovery. I have taken notebooks full of notes and have kept a journal to help me identify my feelings. But I still have two days to grasp all the knowledge I can from the experts in their field. I will make the most of the days I have and learn as much as I possibly can.

Journal entry: "March 6, 2012 – Emotions this morning are tense and agitated. Not sure why unless it is knowing that my stay here is almost over. Will I be okay without the program? How will I react to being put back into the environment that put me here in the first place? I spoke to my social worker today to see exactly when I would be released and she said according to the insurance company, I would be leaving this Friday. She is going to start looking for a therapist for me to use when I leave. It is still hard for me to realize that I am going to have to have a therapist when I leave the program. My feeling about going back to work is that I am not ready – I still have so much to do to get myself back together. After program, I need time to slowly get back into the routine. I want to be home for a while and spend time just being a wife. Ability to take care of my home would be amazing. I think I might be ready to go back to work April 2nd. That will give me three more weeks to get my strength up and be healthier. Look forward to walking this afternoon with Joe. I have to make myself walk every day! I know things are busy at the funeral home, but I know I cannot return right now. Letting go of the guilt is still hard for me. But I have to do what is best for me. Not as tired today as I was yesterday".

Chapter 13

Well, it is day 13 and I am feeling pretty good about the way things have progressed. Goals today include walking 30 minutes and work 1 hour on my scrapbook. Emotions are tired and anxious. I am having thoughts of returning to work and I feel I am just not ready. I am not ready to dive into the day to day grief issues and being around sadness all the time. We spent time this morning talking about loneliness during our meditation reading time. It may be said that the road between loneliness and solitude is the highway to self-esteem. As we begin our journey, most of us fear and flee loneliness. Some people make sure they have plenty of company and continuous talk, lest in the silence they have to hear themselves. When we are alone, we may keep a radio or television going to fill the airwaves. As we come to know and become more comfortable with ourselves, that noise hunger eases up. The disappointing, inadequate self that we always avoided starts to look more interesting – perhaps like someone we would like to spend time with, get to know better. When they are not interrupted, cued, or drowned out, our own thoughts become our most abiding source of challenge, comfort, encouragement, and self-respect. The aloneness is the same whether we are suffering loneliness or enjoying solitude. The magical difference is in our attitude toward ourselves. Getting comfortable with my own company is a sign of growth.

Group one today discussed the Johari window again and how it helps us see ourselves in a new light. Remember I told you earlier that there is an open box, a blind box, a secret box and an unconscious box. The more we store in the secret box the unhealthier we will become. In the open box we feel the safest. It is in this box that we share with others things about our self. The blind box is what others see about me that I don't see. The secret box is where we store things that no one knows or we have shared with no one. The unconscious box is things myself and other are not aware of about me. After lunch we will return to participate in the Johari chair.

The next session was on responding to depression and bi-polar disorder. Triggers were discussed and everyone should recognize them as triggers. The triggers were but not limited to: disappointments, loss, sensory overload (bombardment of stuff), changing of the seasons, rejection (real or perceived), financial problems, problems in relationships, perfectionism, embarrassment or guilt; having too much to do (always feel behind or feel buried), anniversaries of traumatic events; and change in daily routine. We have to identify our own triggers. I believe my triggers are disappointment, loss, embarrassment and guilt and sensory overload. The events in my past such as the sexual abuse caused me to feel embarrassed and guilty. Work had caused sensory overload for me because I was doing everything myself. The loss of my father was the straw that broke the camels' back so to speak. At that time, I had so much bottled up inside me that this loss was the end for me. The fact that I didn't have time to grieve the loss of my father added to the depression. So how do I avoid another episode? There are coping ahead techniques that we must apply to our lives. We must ask our self: What action do I need to take to protect myself? What is the worst thing that could happen? Is there anything I can do to change the situation? What will make me feel better? We must take a daily inventory of our emotions, recognize the warning signs and take action. Warning signs may include: overeating, fatigue, unwillingness to ask for things, low self-esteem, low self-confidence, procrastination, avoiding crowds, irritability, impatience, negative attitude, insecurity, difficulty getting up, insomnia, poor judgment, obsessive thoughts, repeating things, inability to concentrate, suicidal thoughts, paranoia, and lethargy. How do we take action or calm our self? Go for a walk, go swimming, paint, gardening, playing an instrument, puzzles, eating out with a friend or dancing are a few ideas to help take action. Asking for support is very important. First identify a support system, whether it be a close friend, your pastor or family members. Talk to someone every day whether you feel like it or not. There are also a lot of self-help strategies that will help avoid an episode. Journaling, self-help books, peer counseling, taking good care of yourself (like you would take care of your children or your best friend), shift to the positive and keep it simple. Journaling has helped me put my feelings on paper and I can actually hear myself expressing those feelings. Sometimes when I journal my thoughts and feel angry, once I write my feelings down, I don't feel as angry when I finish writing. Getting things off your chest helps relieve stress. It's like writing a letter to someone who has hurt you and never mailing it. You expressed your feelings on paper and feel better.

Group 4 today was the Johari chair participation and I shared! That's right, my time had come and I felt ready to expose myself by sitting in front of the room in the chair. That in itself is an accomplishment. I go into detail about the Johari chair experience in my journal entry.

Journal entry: "March 7, 2012 – Day 13 – Feel tired today, but got a good night's sleep. Joy took me to therapy today and it was good to be able to spend time with her. I am excited about getting better in time to work on wedding plans. I am excited for her and know she deserves the best. Today, I participated in the Johari chair. I felt it would help in my recovery. A chair was placed in the center of the room and the Open time was where the other patients asked me questions. They asked about my children, pets, hobbies, my job and education. These answers were easy for me to answer because they were things that most people knew about me anyway. The next part was the Blind section, where I had to be completely quiet and not respond to their comments. At this moment, I was told that I was strong, educated, good mother, talented, and a survivor. Then it was to the Secret section – wow.

My first thought was am I really ready for this? But I knew I had to in order to let go of some things once and for all. So I began with the fact that I felt very unworthy of their comments and perceptions of me. This is how that went: I feel very unworthy of your wonderful comments and really don't know how to accept them. My inability to accept compliments goes back to 5th grade when Miss Martha would lock me in the closet during recess because I could not memorize the multiplication facts. I was called stupid every day and hit on the head with a ruler. In an attempt to cope, I would literally try and make myself sick every morning to avoid going to school. When that didn't work, I remember running after my dad's car after he dropped me off at school. So my coping skill was to stay in my bedroom, my safe place, and I guess it represented being locked up in that closet. In a sense, I got to where I would enjoy being in the closet to avoid being near the teacher. When I would go to my room, I was always reading. Because of her I have always had a problem with math. From 5th grade, the next problems surfaced in the next few years by living as a "preacher's kid (PK)". I could not do things other kids did because the church members thought "PKs" were to be different. My senior year I dated a boy who was my (or so I thought) soulmate. After 12 ½ months of dating, he just unexpectedly stopped coming to my house. I was devastated to say the least. For 3 months, I sat on the couch waiting for his return, but he never returned. My life was over I thought. Then it was off to Free Will Baptist Bible College and I found myself loving school again. But then I got a part-time job in a print shop owned by one of our church members. First week everything was fine. Then it escalated from rubbing against me to shoulder massages and moved to full blown molestation. This went on for 6 months. He finally moved out of state. Why didn't I tell, because he threatened to destroy my father's ministry and the church? After that I was married to a man I thought loved me. Boy was I wrong – the mental, physical and emotional abuse went on for 13 years. Three children later when he punched my daughter in the face one day, I knew it was time to get out. So I did. Stayed on my own for 6 years. During those six years, I went back to college, raised 2 kids in middle school, 1 in high school and worked 2 jobs. There was no time for me or dating. My father, my best friend, became very ill and was told he had 3-5 years to live. He lived 4 ½ after his diagnosis of myelodysplasia. Myelodysplasia is a type of cancer in which the bone marrow does not make enough healthy blood cells and there are abnormal cells in the blood and/or bone marrow. He had to have blood transfusions, one after another and he became weaker. To watch my best friend deteriorate right before my eyes was heartbreaking. Why did such a good man have to go through so much suffering? I promised daddy that I would do whatever it took to see that the family funeral business did not go under. Then God placed the man of my dreams into my life. He knew what I needed and when. Joe was there for me through Dad's illness and death and has been with me ever since. The promise I made to daddy has probably caused more stress than anything I have ever tried to do. But a promise is a promise. I gave up my teaching career to manage the funeral home. I am around grief and grieving families all the time and I am tired of all the sadness. After sharing in the secret portion of the chair today, I feel as if the shackles have been removed. What a wonderful feeling! It has been 44 years coming. It is never too late to release the events that have haunted us for so many years. Glad I was given the opportunity to do just that. I feel I am getting better".

All these years I had allowed all of these situations in my life to rob me of the joy in living. I can't wait to see what the Lord has in store for the new healthy me.

My Journey With Depression

Chapter 14

I have to tell you yesterday in the Johari chair was exhausting but liberating at the same time. Joe couldn't believe that I shared all the events that I feel led up to my depression. But he was very happy that I did. It's day 14 and one day closer to my being released. Finding peace is so important to me and today our meditation reading was on peace. Anxiety is often our first reaction to conflict, problems, or even our own fears. In those moments, detaching and getting peaceful may seem disloyal or apathetic. We think: If I really care, I'll worry; if this is really important to me, I must stay upset. We convince ourselves that outcomes will be positively affected by the amount of time we spend worrying. Our best problem-solving resource is peace. Solutions arise easily and naturally out of a peaceful state. Often, fear and anxiety block solutions. Anxiety gives power to the problem, not the solution. It does not help to harbor turmoil. Peace is available if we choose it. In spite of chaos and unsolved problems around us, all is well. Things will work out. We can surround ourselves with the resources of the Universe: water, earth, a sunset, a walk, a prayer, a friend. We can relax and let ourselves feel peace. I want to let go of my need to stay in turmoil. Today, I want to cultivate peace and trust that timely solutions and goodness will arise naturally and harmoniously out of the wellspring of peace. I realized today that I must consciously let go and let God.

Session one today was on devising a discharge plan. We made an acrostic that I wanted to share with you in this chapter.

D – doctor appointment, daily schedule, diet, distractions

I – individual therapy (quality time with self once a week), intuitions, identify strengths

S - support group, support system (family, therapist, meetings, church)

C – clear clutter (physical/mental), call someone, control anger, communicate needs

H – help (knowing when to ask), healthy lifestyle, have positive attitude, hobbies

A – attitude, advocate for self, affirmation, attend church

R – rest, recognize triggers, routine, remember your worth it, relaxation techniques

G – goal setting, get involved (church, community activities)

E – energy, exercise, eat healthy, encourage self

P – psychiatrist, pills (take prescribed medications), plan in place, positive thoughts, play time

L – learn something new, loved ones, listen to what body needs or is telling you, laughter, let go

A – avoid triggers, avoid seclusion, appointments

N – no negative thoughts, never underestimate yourself

I must have a plan in place in order to make it beyond these walls. My toolbox is now filled with strategies and techniques to help me cope with the depression. We are 100% responsible for our well-being. That is a little scary for me since I made such a mess of it before coming to program. I keep telling myself, "I can do this".

The next session was on the roles children play in the family. Before this discussion, I never thought that there were certain roles played out by each member of the family. The first role is the family hero. This child is the fixer, protector, becomes the adult keeps the family looking good. As a result, this child experiences a loss of self and is out of touch with his or her feelings. Next is the scapegoat. This is the "bad" kid, trouble, poor grades, defiant, acts out, and keeps focus off the family. He serves as the distractor. The results are loss of self, out of touch with feelings, and more risk of alcohol/drug abuse. Then we have the mascot: class clown, fun kid, jokes, laughs, life of the party, keeps everyone happy, takes pressure off family and diffuses the real problems. The result of the mascot is loss of self, out of touch with their feelings. Finally we have the lost child. This child is quiet, keeps to self, withdrawn, least likely to get help they need because of being too quiet and no trouble. They too experience loss of self and out of touch with their feelings. After this discussion, I labeled myself as the family hero. I am the go to person when something needs doing. I make it my mission to always keep the family looking good. This is what led to my depression. I was afraid of missing up the perfect little family that people perceived us to be. After all, we were the preacher's family and everyone knows that we were perfect or supposed to be. So I could not go around telling people of my past and letting them see my true feelings. It just wouldn't look good for the family.

The next session was on spiritual recovery. Actually they called it our spiritual "un-covery". It is not necessarily about religion; it is about uncovering the good qualities we have at our core. Instead of feeling that we have to adopt new qualities, we need to see that we already have these qualities in abundance. We need to form new attitudes, beliefs, and habits that will help us know the truth about ourselves. Spiritual recovery helps us move toward the truth about ourselves – that we're created perfect and need to let that perfection shine through. Knowing this truth, we can then form new practices, beliefs, and ways of thinking that will help us move away from the darkness of our depression or whatever we are dealing with and move toward the light of recovery. Spiritual recovery helps us change our thinking and feeling so we are no longer weighted down with feelings of shame, guilt, or fear. We may still feel these things when we make a mistake. But we will no longer believe that we are wrong. Instead, we'll come to see that while we make mistakes, at our very core we are good. This simple idea – that our very nature is good, rather than flawed, evil or bad – can and will change our view of the world, ourselves and our lives. My spiritual recovery has been allowing God back into my life. I know that no matter what has happened in the past, God loves me and has always been there for me even when I turned my back on him.

The song "Redeemed" by Big Daddy Weave sums up the way I feel.

> Seems like all I could see was the struggle
> Haunted by ghosts that lived in my past
> Bound up in shackles of all my failures
> Wondering how long is this gonna last
> Then you look at this prisoner and say to me "son
> Stop fighting a fight it's already been won".
>
> I am redeemed. You set me free
> So I'll shake off these heavy chains
> Wipe away every stain, now I'm not who I used to be
> I am redeemed, I am redeemed.
>
> All my life I have been called unworthy
> Named by the voice of my shame and regret
> But when I hear you whisper, "child lift up your head"
> I remember, oh God, You're not done with me yet.

Because I don't have to be the old man inside of me
'Cause his day is long dead and gone
Because I've got a new name, a new life, I'm not the same
And a hope that will carry me home.

I am redeemed, you set me free
So I'll shake off these heavy chains
Wipe away every stain, yeah, I'm not who I used to be
Oh, God I'm not who I used to be
Jesus, I'm not who I used to be
Cause I am redeemed
Thank God, redeemed.

Journal entry: "March 8, 2012 – Day 14: My devotion was make a decision and turn our will and our lives over to the care of God. Emotions wise I feel rested and very good. I am still scared about leaving the program, but I think it will be alright. Kind of sad to think tomorrow I will be released from this facility. How will I react to the pressures of life and my job? My goal is to take one day at a time and be the best I can be that day. Beginning to show signs of moving from passive to assertive. Plan on getting more assertive. Learned today that the role in my family was the family hero. Always making sure everyone is okay and in the process I have lost me. I texted Chris this afternoon to tell him the plans for recovery and checked to see if I would get paid while off. His response was "you are out of sick and vacation days". I became very upset wondering what on earth Joe and I are going to do. We simply cannot live on what Joe brings home. I was so upset that I went straight to bed when I got home. Going back to my old coping skills. Hide from the problem, Sheila. That made me mad to feel that way. Got out of bed at 6:30 p.m. to visit Joy, Noah, and Ruthie. Joe tells me not to worry, but that is easier said than done. Going to bed at 9 p.m. and hope that tomorrow is a better day".

My Journey With Depression

Chapter 15

This day has finally come. My final day in the program. My goal for today is to make it through the day without breaking down, journaling at least one page and again walk for 30 minutes. Emotions today are everywhere. I feel defeated, upset, and anxious and I have a headache. Quote from the morning meditation reading by Andre Berthiaume: "We all wear masks, and the time comes when we cannot remove them without removing some of our own skin". Over the past three weeks, I feel like I have started to peel away at the masks I have been hiding behind all these years. The peeling of skin allows new skin to shine through and with new skin comes new life. We wear masks to hide our real faces from those around us and even from ourselves. There are seductive masks, innocent masks, white knight masks, tough guy masks, black sheep masks, lone wolf masks, and many more. Sometimes we want to take on another identity so others will not see our insecurities. Or we think taking the form of someone else will give us power over others, or they will like us better, or we can escape ourselves. The cost of wearing a mask is not getting a chance to develop our real personalities. I have hid behind masks to cover the bruises and scars of the events in my life. I have been hiding all my life and didn't even realize it until now. Lord, help me to have the courage to drop my phony masks in order to grow stronger in self-knowledge.

Leaving the program is very scary for me and the other patients that will be leaving today. Session one the discussion was on self-destructing coping skills. I don't want to waste what I have learned in the program when I get back home. I don't what to undo the progress that I have made these three weeks.

There are seven self-destructing coping skills we need to be aware of and avoid at all costs:

1. Spend time thinking about the past pain, mistakes and problems.

2. Suicidal thoughts and attempting suicide.

3. Isolating yourself to avoid pain and excessive sleeping.

4. Avoid dealing with causes of the problems.

5. Drug and alcohol use, overeating/under eating, self-harming, gambling, shopping excessively.

6. Surrender to your pain and live an unfulfilling life.

7. Putting your life on hold to take care of others.

If we allow these things to come back into our life it will cost us: missing out on the present, good things that might be happening which leads to regret that leads to depression. There will be physical problems as well: possible death, hospitalization, shame, isolating self, poor self-esteem, quilt, seizures and other medical issues. This all leads to more pain, more depression, loneliness and family relationship problems. It is a cycle of unhappiness, cheating yourself, staying depressed and in pain and live a life of regret. The only person you can change is you. This mental illness of depression has caused me to seclude myself from others and have feelings of anger. In our discussion we had to think about times we felt good about our self. I feel good about myself when I have no headache and I am spending time with my husband, children and grandchildren. I feel good about myself when I am working on a special project like a scrapbook or cross-stitching. But lately, I have put all that on hold and consumed myself with work. Some of the things I have gotten from this program is that we are not guaranteed tomorrow, so don't worry about tomorrow. Live each day to the fullest. Don't sweat the small stuff. We can't change the past, can't know the future, so we missed the present. As time goes on things will become clearer. Don't beat yourself up if you slip, pick yourself up and get back on track. It's okay – don't let it be your excuse to go back to old patterns.

Journal entry: "March 9, 2012 This morning I feel as if I have been kicked in the stomach – deflated. Knowing that what is best for me is to return to work April 2, but I have been told I will not receive my salary from today until April 2. How will Joe and I make it? How will the house and car note get paid? Who will put food on our table? Joe is only working part-time and can't find a full time job, so my income paid the big bills. They say let go and let God... I am trying but the days ahead look black from where I am standing. After everything I have done for the funeral home, everything I have sacrificed, the problems I have due partly because of my job and when I need them I'm on my own – no help. I feel myself going into that seclusion mode. Last night after hearing the news, I went straight to bed. God, help me! Was very quiet on my way to therapy. Mom tried to make conversation, but I was not in the mood to talk. Posted on Facebook this morning, "This morning I feel like I have been kicked while I'm down. I feel trapped and pray God hears my prayers today. I need his intervention in several worries I have today". How will I make it? For some reason the only safe place for me is the partial hospitalization program. Here I can be myself and worries seem to disappear. I know that is not the real world and that I have to face problems head on. Everyone in group can see a change in me today. I just want to cry. I feel things building up and I feel like I did when I first started the group. God, I place all my cares and worries on you. Group has been good today. Topics of discussion were things I really needed to hear. Spoke to the psychiatrist about how I felt about leaving – apprehensive, scared and helpless. He told me to take one day at a time and not do anything that would make me relapse. The wrap up today was very sad for me. As everyone gave me well wishes, I began to cry. These people I had grown to love like family that really understood me and I could be myself around. Several wished me happiness and peace, others prayed that I find what I really want to do with my life, and others told me how strong they thought I was for coming out of past events with a caring heart. Before I left, I talked to my social worker. She hugged me and told me to hang in there and begin to enjoy life. She said I had made so much progress since day one. As I walked outside, I became nauseated. As I turned the handle to the black gate, I had come and gone through for the last three weeks, my heart sank. It became real – I was on my own. I began to sob – I felt all alone and like there was nowhere to go. Mother picked me up and I said nothing to her the whole way home. Tomorrow is another day – just hope it will be better emotionally for me. What do I really want to do with my life? Now that is the big question".

Chapter 16

The program is really over and I am now on my own. There is a great big world out there and I am still not sure I will be able to cope with all of the arsenal that life has to launch at me every day. There is one thing I do know and that is I have been given the tools to make that return into the real world as easy as possible. It is now up to me, the work is just beginning and if I want to get healthier emotionally, mentally, spiritually and physically I better get to work. Along this journey, I have found out that I am really stronger than I once thought. The most important thing I learned in program was that I am worthy of the greatest life possible. Since leaving the program, I have had more good days than bad. The recovery process is an ongoing day to day process. Not every day will be filled with rainbows and flowers. Life is not perfect, it is hard. When reading my journal entries the days and weeks beyond the program, I see a woman who has a renewed lease on life. She is not the same woman that laid in the hospital bed for four days in a fetal position with no recollection of her family and friends. This new woman found the courage to leave her job at the funeral home and return to her love of teaching. This new woman had the courage and strength to go back to school and receive her Master's in Educational Leadership and has published two books. She is able to share her life's story with the world and not be ashamed any more of what people think or how people will react. This woman did share her feeling with her family. I want to share a letter I wrote to them.

March 24, 2012

Joe, Mom, Joy, Joseph, Terry, Christi:

This letter is being written to every member of my family. As a part of my recovery, it was suggested by my therapist that I write this to you. I have a mental illness. Just like alcoholics, I will always have a mental illness. I know that is scary for you and it certainly wasn't something I wanted to hear. Each day I am learning ways to cope with the illness.

On February 8, 2012 my body said enough is enough and it snapped. I woke up with a severe migraine on February 7th and that was the last thing I remembered until February 14th. Joe found me passed out in the bathroom floor and took me to the emergency room. Doctors ran every test imaginable and concluded that my problem was psychological. They said my body was shutting down and telling me it was over. I was a pressure cooker, with bad events and memories stuffed inside and finally the top blew off. Losing my memory and not recognizing each of you was a scary feeling and I am sorry to have put you through that, but I had no control. Being told I was going to have to go to a psychiatric hospital was humiliating and scary to say the least.

During my stay in the adult partial hospitalization program at Vanderbilt Psychiatric Hospital, I learned a lot about myself. Learning why I was the way I was turned out to be enlightening. It also opened up wounds that I had covered up for years. While in therapy, I learned that I was a passive individual. By being passive, I do not stand up for myself, I am a people pleaser, and I put others first. I am insecure and have a lack of confidence. I am lonely, sad and dissatisfied with my life. I let others make choices for me. My first question was, "How does someone become passive?" This is where the group therapy came in and helped me pinpoint the answers.

In therapy with my psychiatrist, we started back to my earliest childhood memories and worked forward. My life was perfect until 5th grade. The events that took place in 5th grade haunt me to this day. The events began my journey into depression. In 5th grade, I was locked in a closet every day during recess because I had problems learning my multiplication facts. I was called stupid and hit on the head several times a day with a wooden ruler. I survived with the wounds to prove it. I felt defeated, worthless, stupid and all alone. This led me to stay in my room all the time reading. If I was stupid, then I had to read everything I could get my hands on to make me smart. Being closed off in my room was the only way I felt safe. Life went on. I remember being told by people that I never smiled and always looked so unhappy. At that point in my life there was nothing to smile or be happy about.

Things got better with time for a while. The only problems were staying out of the target of the church members. They were always finding us doing something wrong. So again, to make sure I didn't do anything to jeopardize dad's position in the church, I secluded myself in my room. I thought if I didn't leave my room, I could not get into trouble. High school came and I remember mom asking me why I wasn't dating anyone. This was my senior year. My first thought was is there something wrong with me? Was I supposed to be dating? Up until that point, I thought I was living a normal life. The only boy I would consider dating finally asked me out. We were together day and night. He was the love of my life, so I thought. I was sure he was my soulmate. We had discussed marriage after he got out of college and began making plans for our future together. Then one night, without any notice, he walked out of my life to the arms of a girl ten years older than he. Again my life was pulled out from under me. I felt stupid again and wondered what was wrong with me. Why didn't he love me? I spent the next three months sitting on the couch staring out the window waiting for his return. During that time, I lost 30 pounds and only left the house to go to church.

Then it was off to Free Will Baptist Bible College. Finally, I felt accepted for me. While at Bible College, I was offered a part-time job in a printing shop owned by a man in our church. I worked every afternoon from 1 to 5. The first week was fine, but then things began to happen. The nightmare began to happen. This man molested me every day for 6 months. I told him to stop, but he said he was the boss and I had to do what he said. He would do this after everyone else left the building. He told me if I ever told anyone that my father would never preach again in any church. So to protect dad, I didn't say anything. You may be thinking, why did I continue to go back each day. He threatened me and would drive to the college to make sure I was there. While all of this was going on, I led my life as if nothing happened. I told no one. So one more nasty event was stored away in the pressure cooker, but I never forgot it and how it made me feel. Yes, by this time my self-esteem was nonexistent.

I transferred to Austin Peay State University in 1977. During that time, I met the man that would become my husband. He began to control me. I think I allowed it because I really wanted to believe that I was worthy of someone's love and attention. He would come to school and visit me in the dorm every day and would get mad if I had studying or something else to do. He put so much pressure on me that I had to quit school. We married, but was anything but happily ever after. Three beautiful children is the only good thing that came from that marriage. I was verbally, emotionally, and physically abused by him. He told me that I would never be able to live without him. He told dad one time that the only thing he could say good about me was that I was a good mother to his children. Whatever self-esteem had begun to surface was quickly gone. His temper was explosive and he hit anything in his path whether it be a wall, a door, me or Joy. After 13 years, I had enough and left the day he hit Joy and verbally abused Joseph.

I found myself with three children to raise. Without the love and support of my parents, I would have never made it. I worked two jobs and went back to college and raised three children. I feel guilty for all the things Joy, Joseph and Terry missed out on because I just did not have the money. I hope you know that I love you more than life itself and everything I did, I did for you. In 2000,

I graduated from Austin Peay and began teaching. I loved my job and felt good about myself for accomplishing my degree.

Joe came along and for the very first time in my life, I experienced true love. God sent him to me at the perfect time. You all know how much I love him. He has always treated me with love, respect and support. On January 26, 2005 at 5:30 a.m. my life was once again turned upside down. Dad, my best friend, was gone. His death left me numb inside and the grief was too much to bear. But I had to deal with it and get back to work and go on. For a while I taught school and was on call at the funeral home.

Prior to Dad's weakening condition, he and I talked one night in the hospital about the business. He did not want mom to be taken advantage of by some businessmen trying to buy the funeral home. Right there, I promised dad that I would do whatever it took to keep the business running as long as mother wanted it and to protect her. I never intended to still be there 7 years later. I gave up teaching and became the manager of the funeral home. Basically, I was on call 24/7, met with families, did all the paperwork, worked funerals and some visitations, sold preneed and monuments. And during that time I had to find time to be with Joe, my children and grandchildren. Talk about pressure, the funeral business is not meant for one person to do it all. Mother does what she can and I know she feels overwhelmed at times.

My migraines increased, I was finding myself in bed all day on my days off and weekends. I began to dread going to work. I was burnt out. I began to resent my job and became mad because I had no help and just wanted to run away and never come back. Two weeks before our cruise, I began having trouble remembering things. I was having 2 and 3 migraines each week and they were getting more intense. My body was tired and I had no energy. The cruise was wonderful and I felt alive and happy again. The minute the plane landed back in Nashville, I began to feel my body tense. It never left. Returning to work as usual was my plan. My memory and concentration were gone. I lashed out at a state preneed auditor because I thought he had missed our appointment. Later, I realized I thought it was Wednesday when actually it was a Tuesday. Other things began to happen – I misplaced things, became angry with people and my emotions were a wreck. Then it happened, I snapped. After hospitalization and being told I had to be admitted into the adult partial hospitalization program, I was humiliated. As I walked into the building for the first time, I felt all alone and like that little girl in 5ᵗʰ grade being punished for being stupid. How could I not see this coming? Why didn't I see depression surfacing? Why would I since I was great in keeping things to myself and going on with life.

I am thankful for the program, the social workers, therapist and psychiatrist for giving me a second chance at a happy life. They taught me it was my job to take care of myself. Being able to share my emotions and thoughts each day with the group was refreshing. I finally felt that what I said and felt really mattered. I am learning that I do deserve to be happy. I am taking one day at a time to recover and learn to deal with everything that has happened in my life. Now my days begins with a devotion and prayer time, readings from two meditational books and writing in my journal. That is "me" time. As I begin to peel away layers of my life, I see how past events have molded me into the person I am today. I want to feel good, enjoy life and be happy. I realize now that I have to confront my past, let it go and travel this journey of recovery on my own.

I do realize that this is all new to all of you. I am asking each of you to be patient with me. There may be days that I just can't talk or deal with things. If that happens, I will tell you, not today. I hope you can all respect that. I have to set boundaries, say no, and change an old pattern. I am aware that I will probably get flak from some people, but that is okay. I will no longer let other people's reactions control me, stop me or influence my decision to take care of me. My family's support is very important in this journey. I am scared. There are good days and there are bad days still, but I am trying to cope. I am not well even though people think and say I look good. Mental illness is not understood and those of us with it look okay on the outside. But inside we are broken. It's not a broken leg where you see a cast or cancer where you see a bald head from chemo. Mental illness has no outward appearances most of the time.

I am not sure where my journey will lead me. The doctors feel that I cannot go back to the funeral home and do what I had been doing. They predict that if I do, I will be back the way I was within three months. So April 2nd, I will go back to the funeral home beginning one day a week and working up to four or five days a week. When I return, there will have to be changes made and conditions will have to be heard and respected. I cannot and will not allow my life to be taken from me again. I am working so hard to turn back now. Please understand I love all of you and need all of you in my life. I need your love, prayers, support and respect. I know I am on the right path and pray that God will show me where I need to be and what I need to do with my life. Change scares me a little bit, but I understand it has to happen in order to recover.

Love,

Sheila

I want to share with you a story about the chicken and the eagle. This is a story about chickens and one very confused eagle. As you read it, think about life from the eagle's perspective. Can you relate?

One day a naturalist who was passing by a chicken farm was struck with curiosity. He noticed an eagle, the king of all birds, living among the chickens. He asked the farmer, "Why do you have this eagle confined to live in the barnyard with the chickens?

"Since I have given it chicken feed and trained it to be a chicken, it has never learned to fly," replied the farmer. "It behaves as chickens behave, so it is no longer an eagle."

"Still," insisted the naturalist, "it has the heart of an eagle and can surely be taught to fly."

After taking it over, the two men agreed to find out whether this was possible. Gently, the naturalist took the eagle in his arms and said, "You belong to the sky and not the earth. Stretch forth your wings and fly."

The eagle, however, was confused: he did not know who he was. He was comfortable with his life and was content with the farmer providing his food and being in the company of the chickens. Seeing the chickens eating their food, he jumped down to be with them again.

Undismayed, the naturalist took the eagle on the following day up on the roof of the house and urged him again, saying, "You are an eagle. Stretch forth your wings and fly." But the eagle was afraid of his unknown self. He was afraid of the world he did not know. He was scared to fly. He jumped down once more for the chicken food.

On the next day, the naturalist rose early and took the eagle out of the barnyard to a high mountain. There he held the king of birds high above him and encouraged him again, saying, "You are an eagle. You belong to the sky as well as the earth. Stretch forth your wings now and fly."

The eagle looked back toward the barnyard. Then he looked up to the sky. He still did not fly.

Then the naturalist lifted him straight toward the sun. The eagle looked up to the sky and began to tremble. Slowly he began to stretch his wings. He look back once more to the barnyard and then fixed his gaze toward the sky. At last … With a triumphant cry he soared into the heavens.

From that moment on, the eagle was living life as an eagle. Now it may be that the eagle still remembers the chickens with a certain fondness and nostalgia. It may even be that the occasionally revisits the barnyard. But as far as anyone knows, he has never returned to the barnyard to live the life of chicken. He truly was an eagle, even though he has lived the life of a chicken.

Just like this eagle, people who have learned to think of themselves as something they are not can re-decide in favor of what they really are.

So this is the story. A story about accepting ourselves as less than what we could be. About living life without taking risks and experiencing our true potential. We think we are chickens because we have accepted a perception about ourselves that is less than our capabilities. In truth, we are eagles with the potential to soar, to be free to experience our true essence. But we often find ourselves in the barnyard feeling safe and fearful. We often feel no sense of life's purpose or direction.

Are you stretching your wings? I want to encourage you today that you are an eagle. You may have been brought up in situations and experiences that limited your understanding of your potential. I sure did. But it's time now for the past to lose its hold on you. Don't die a chicken. Soar high, just as you were meant to. Be all that you were meant to be.

www.ingramcontent.com/pod-product-compliance
Lightning Source LLC
Chambersburg PA
CBHW050542280326
41933CB00011B/1681